ALPHA VIRTUS

EXALTED MASCULINE ARCHETYPE
ABBREVIATED FIELD GUIDE

ALPHA VIRTUS

ROBERT ALTHUIS

ALPHA VIRTUS
Exalted Masculine Archetype Abbreviated Field Guide
First Edition

ISBN 979-8-9929664-3-5 *Hardcover*
979-8-9929664-2-8 *Paperback*
979-8-9929664-4-2 *Ebook*

Published by Love+Truth Publishing

To my Maple Leaf

*For lovingly devoting your exquisite Feminine
essence, grace, and wisdom to my attunement
to the teachings within this book.*

*Our "One Beast" transcends time and space and will
never be undone, no matter where the plot lines of
our stories might have us journey in this lifetime.*

*Your fingerprints are forever etched upon me,
and I am a better man for it.*

CONTENTS

THE SIDDHIS

THE ATTUNEMENT

May this book lose all its relevancy in a brief time as a product of humanity rising to meet its highest potential.

— R A

PREFACE

ALPHA & OMEGA
The Sacred Journey of Mastery & Integration

Every journey has a beginning and an end, and so does the Grand Odyssey of our Soul throughout eternity. Every man walks a path between Alpha and Omega—between initiation and completion, between the awakening of his potential and its full embodiment.

The title *Alpha Virtus* is not intended to be a reference to the so-called "Alpha male"—that limited cultural narrative that has reduced the idea of the "Alpha" to dominance, power, and status in a social hierarchy. Instead, this book refers to the true meaning of Alpha, something far more grand and profound: *The Beginning,* the first spark of mastery—Alpha is the moment of initiation into something higher.

In the ancient world, Alpha & Omega represented the entirety of existence—both the first and the last, the origin and the culmination. Yet, beyond its significance as a symbol of totality, Alpha & Omega also represents the Sacred Polarity—the Masculine and Feminine principles that govern all of Life. Alpha is the Divine Masculine; Omega is the Divine Feminine. Together, they are the primordial forces that animate the sacred dance of creation, the interplay between structure and flow, action and receptivity, discipline and grace.

This book is about initiation into the exalted Masculine. *Alpha Virtus* is not about reaching a final destination of manhood; it is about stepping onto the path of attunement—aligning with the highest virtues, embodying the sanctified Masculine archetype, and walking with unwavering integrity in each moment.

But initiation is only half the journey.

The second book in this series, *Omega Sattva*, will complete this arc—guiding the man who has mastered the virtues into his full integration with the Feminine. If *Alpha Virtus* is initiation, *Omega Sattva* is transcendence—the graduation into the final stage of embodiment, where the exalted Masculine and the exalted Feminine merge into wholeness. This mirrors the ancient rites of passage taught in the mystery schools, where the final resurrection of the initiate required the alchemy of both energies, just as the Christos-Sophia union represents the fusion of Divine Wisdom with Divine Love.

The path between Alpha & Omega is not linear. It is not measured in worldly success or accolades. It is measured in the depth of a man's *Being*—in who he chooses to be in every moment.

And so, this book is not for the man who waits. It is for the man who chooses. The man who steps forward. The man who commits to the venerable path of initiation.

This is the sacred path—from Alpha to Omega, from Initiation to Integration, from Masculine to Wholeness.

The Grand Odyssey starts here.

INTRODUCTION

This book is dedicated to men—and men only. While it has much to offer boys, women, and girls, who I wholeheartedly invite and encourage to read these pages, you are not men. Boys are not men—at least not yet—and women and girls will never know what it is to be a man.

Men are born as raw diamonds: unpolished, unrefined, and with unrealized potential and value. Over the course of their lifetimes, these raw diamonds are cut, formed, shaped, and molded through an endless process of inculcation into manhood. This initiation is forged in the fires of challenges, burdens, and pressures.

But a man's task is not merely to avoid cracking or falling apart under pressure—that is mere survival. His mission is far greater. He must rise above the trials of life, above the constraints of his circumstances, and most of all, above himself and the pulls of his primal nature. He may come to be loved, but his ultimate reward is respect—a respect that can only be earned. Hence, his journey is not meant or designed to be one of comfort, convenience, hand-outs, or freebies, whether from Nature or society, as neither allows him to earn the respect he so deeply craves.

There are immutable laws that govern our Universe, and all of Creation operates in accordance with this law and order. The intelligence of Life itself—the Grand Architecture—is infinitely brilliant and flawless in its design. Within this cosmic order, the Masculine archetype holds a unique and invaluable place, just as the Feminine archetype does. They are inherently equal in worth and importance yet vastly different in their purpose, roles, innate qualities, and significance as aspects of Source Consciousness or the Godhead or Creator if you will.

Yet, in today's world—a world rife with wars, violence, hate, oppression, racism, inequality, injustice, corruption, and environmental degradation—the Masculine, embodied by men, is often villainized. Many view it as the root cause of the very ugliness that plagues our planet. And regrettably, there is some truth to this perspective.

Yet, while this perspective is understandable, it is incomplete. It fails to recognize that what we have witnessed throughout history—expressed by men through acts of dominance, violence, and greed—is not the true Masculine archetype. Rather, it is a shadow of the Masculine, a distorted reflection by mortal men of the exalted Masculine archetype. Masculinity is not the villain; it is the antidote. Indeed, it is the only solution.

This book serves as a roadmap for men to ascend into the true Masculine archetype, a divine blueprint encoded into their very DNA. It is an invitation to remember who we truly are—at our core—so that we may finally lay to rest the identity crisis that has haunted mortal men since the dawn of civilization.

This book is about respect.

Not the respect of others or society, but respect from the Creator—the source in whose image man was made. The pilgrimage into manhood, as a reflection of the truthful Masculine archetype, is the ultimate purpose of any man walking this earthly realm. Everything else is a detail, insignificant in the face of the one Infinite Game the Universe has been playing since eternity began.

Here's the Truth: When we—mortal men—earn the respect of the Creator, the dynastic keys to this Universe are placed in our stewardship. Respect from others will follow effortlessly because the true essence of the Masculine archetype is undeniable. It transcends culture, upbringing, or ideology. All men, women, and children—no matter how deeply lost in their identity crises—instinctively recognize the energy of true Masculinity when they encounter it. It touches something primal and universal within us all.

A man who embodies the true Masculine archetype touches the souls of all who encounter him. His Power extends far beyond the shallow metrics of "power and influence" that our confused world clings to. What society mistakenly calls power—money, wealth, titles, status, connections, resources, physical strength, or military might—is not Power at all. These are merely instruments of Force. And Force, by its very nature, is dependent on a medium to exist. This is how we can always distinguish Force from true Power.

True Power requires no medium, or in other words no form, vehicle, instrument, or mechanism. It simply is. Truth carries Power; lies, by contrast, demand Force to sustain themselves. Love wields infinite Power, whereas hate and prejudice must be propped up by constant effort. Freedom flows effortlessly from Power, but oppression can only exist through the relentless application of Force.

The ethos of the Masculine archetype, as revealed in this book, is the path for any man to rise into his true Power.

But this Power is not freely given. A man must earn it. He must face and conquer his inner dragons, master the tendencies of his lower nature, and transcend himself. The embodiment of the true Masculine archetype is not bestowed—it is forged. It will not come easily, nor should it. Every step of the way is arduous, and he will be tested time and again. Yet, deep down, he wouldn't want it any other way because he understands this fundamental Truth: respect cannot be claimed for anything that hasn't been earned.

If you, my brother, choose to read this book and commit to putting its principles into practice, then you will officially become an Initiate. But let me be clear: becoming an Initiate is only the beginning. It is meaningless unless you also take on the weighty burden of absolute accountability and responsibility for your life. This is your sacred rite of passage into manhood—a journey to embody the true Masculine archetype within the Grand Architecture of all Creation.

No one can walk this path for you. It is yours alone. And with that comes the responsibility for everything in your life—the good, the bad, the ugly, and the sublime. If it exists in your world, it is yours to own. No more excuses. No more passing blame, pointing fingers, or succumbing to victimhood. No more tolerating mediocrity when a higher potential is within your grasp.

The beauty lies in this Truth: You were designed and built for this journey. As you walk this sacred path, you will come to treasure the discovery of your own capacity and purpose—a revelation that will illuminate every corner of your life.

Read on only if you are ready to embark on this rite of passage. The words within this book are not for entertainment purposes, nor will they provide the warm fuzziness of spiritual platitudes or cliché teachings that lack depth and substance. This book was written to confront the deep slumber prevalent among men who have not yet escaped boyhood, yet something deep within is yearning to embody their manhood. Their Soul is stirring, and what they are craving is exactly what the world is craving for in them. If this is you, know this book was designed to awaken a deep remembrance within you. And once awakened, this Truth cannot be lulled back to sleep.

Once you see, you cannot unsee.

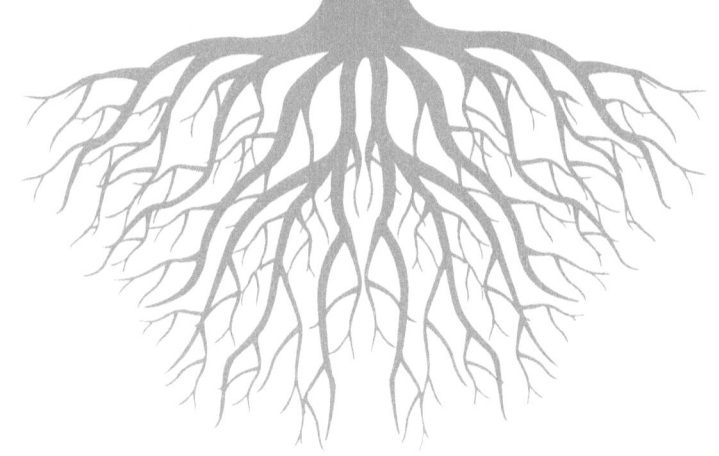

THE CONTEXT

"The superior man thinks always of virtue, the common man thinks of comfort."

—CONFUCIUS

LOST IN A
SEA OF CHANGE

S INCE THE DAWN OF CIVILIZATION, HUMANITY—
and the societies it has built—has been largely male-
oriented and male-dominated. Not truly Masculine, as
will become evident, but male. This dynamic was neither wholly
right nor wrong, but it offered a balance of power that was, at
the very least, clear. And clarity, as we'll see, is an essential ingre-
dient of Order.

Without Order, Chaos takes hold. Chaos brings with it
degeneration and degradation. Things unravel, rot, and decay
until they eventually perish—that is the natural consequence of

Chaos. Today, we find ourselves firmly rooted within this realm of Chaos, especially in Western civilization. The root of this Chaos? Confusion. And confusion is nothing more than the long shadow cast by a lack of clarity.

Yet, within the heart of Chaos lies the seed of Order. This is one of the immutable laws that govern our Universe. As Greek philosopher Heraclitus observed: "Nothing is; everything is always becoming." Just as day turns into night and night into day, there is a rhythm and cadence to all of Creation. Chaos, far from being purely destructive, serves a necessary purpose. It clears the field, tills the soil, and creates fertile ground for new growth. Out of the seeming cataclysms, destruction, and even death of Chaos emerges something better—something more evolved, more complex, and more intelligent—a new cycle in the eternal Infinite Game played by the Universe.

This is where we find ourselves today: *lost in a sea of change.* The old world is dying, while the new has yet to fully reveal itself. We are trapped in a transitional phase where confusion reigns supreme. Yet, there is reason for hope—we are nearing the end of this passage. Soon, we will emerge from this long, dark tunnel into the light of what comes next.

How can I be so sure?

Because Chaos is orgasmic in nature. It builds tension and pressure, layer upon layer until it reaches a breaking point. Then, like a volcano, it erupts—spilling its molten force outward. But as the eruption subsides, what follows is the rapture of rebirth, renewal, growth, and expansion.

Truth is often a bitter tonic, but any good doctor knows that to heal a festering wound, the bandage must first come off. The wound must be exposed to oxygen and cleaned thoroughly before applying healing agents that support the body's innate intelligence. This intelligence is designed to heal, repair, and regenerate itself—from the moment of conception until your very last breath.

Falsehoods, on the other hand, are like malignant bacteria. They infect and disrupt the energetic coherence of the body, what medicine calls homeostasis. When this coherence is broken, illness or dysfunction sets in. But unlike physical pathogens, Falsehoods operate on the mental plane. They infect thoughts, beliefs, and perceptions, throwing the mind into a state of dissonance.

Truth is like oxygen, and the primary healing agents for the mental plane are Awareness, Intelligence, Love, and Compassion. When I speak of intelligence, I refer not to the limited human concept of IQ but to the intelligence of Life itself—the vast, orchestrating force that animates and directs all of Creation. Humanity's fixation on IQ as the pinnacle of intelligence is a fundamental misunderstanding—one we'll explore and dispel fully in the chapter on Wisdom.

Everything in our Universe is a fractal of something greater. We exist in a fractal-based reality, where each part reflects the whole. Sacred geometry serves as the architecture and engineering of this reality, with Consciousness as its fundamental fabric. This Consciousness manifests itself into a holographic reality—"that" which we experience as our "material" world—by taking on the particle state of quanta—subatomic particles. In its wave state, this same Consciousness becomes what we refer to as the formless or unmanifest "ether," "space," or "nothingness" all around us. But this "nothingness" is far from empty. More so than a vacuum, it is, in fact, a plenum—an infinite field brimming with energy in its wave state, rich with potential and vitality.

Falsehoods, as previously noted, reside and operate on the mental plane. They can be most easily understood as ideas, ideologies, theories, beliefs, and other psychological constructs that conflict with the intelligence of Life itself. Truth, by contrast, encompasses all those constructs that align with this intelligence. The intelligence of Life itself is the same as the Grand Architecture of Creation—these terms are interchangeable. It is, in essence, extraordinarily simple and straightforward. When seen clearly, there is no confusion.

So far, so good.

The physical body exists on the physical or material plane and is nested within the emotional plane, which in turn is nested within the mental plane, followed by the spiritual plane, and ultimately the cosmic plane. Each of these planes serves a distinct purpose, yet they are all fractals of a greater whole. At the pinnacle of this fractal hierarchy is Source Consciousness—the Absolute. What's far more important to grasp here is not what it's called, but what it is. What we're pointing at and referring to as this "pinnacle" is truly a singularity within which everything (i.e. all fractals) exists and from which all that has ever existed, exists today, or will ever exist in the future was originated, created, and born. Every fractal within this singularity that is the Absolute is a reflection of its origin: the infinite and divine Source.

This Absolute—which we could also call Singularity—goes by many names like God, Creator, Monad, Yahweh, Allah, Tao, Brahman, The All, Oversoul, Great Spirit, Tagaloa, Manitou, Universal Mind, Infinite Intelligence, Source Consciousness, and the list goes on and on. Words are just linguistic labels, though they are never the "thing" itself. Words, which are part of language, can only point at something, so it makes no difference what word you prefer. Use whichever one strikes your fancy. Just know that when I use any of these labels, what I am really pointing at is Divinity.

If everything in our Universe is a fractal of this Absolute, and this Absolute is of a Divine nature, then all fractals within this Universe must also be of a Divine nature. It cannot be any other way, as nothing exists outside of this singularity that is the Absolute. By definition, everything exists within and is derived from this Absolute.

We, as humans, are fractals of the Absolute, which means our true nature must be Divinity itself. In fact, everything within the world of form is of divine origin. This universal Truth is encapsulated in the Hermetic axiom: "*While All is in The All, it is equally true that The All is in All.*" In other words, just as all of Creation resides within the Creator, the Creator resides within every part of Creation.

Let us be clear about our purpose here: to systematically eradicate confusion by illuminating universal Truth and thereby distilling clarity from murky waters. The Chaos of being "lost in a sea of change" stems from confusion. Clarity is our compass, and it will guide us to safe harbor. That harbor is none other than the Grand Architecture of all Creation—the divine blueprint of our Cosmos.

When we, as individuals or as a collective, align ourselves with the Grand Architecture of Creation—or the intelligence of Life itself—we enter into coherence with our true nature: Divinity. This exalted state of *Being* mirrors the concept of homeostasis within the body. Just as our physical body is governed by an innate intelligence that constantly works to heal, repair, and regenerate, so too does this higher intelligence seek to restore coherence wherever there is dissonance.

Falsehoods create dissonance on the mental plane, while Truth restores coherence. Chaos springs from dissonance, and Order emerges when coherence is reestablished.

How do we recognize Order?

It's simple. Life itself provides the evidence. Order allows life to thrive, prosper, grow, and expand. It makes life bloom, blossom, regenerate, and create beauty in countless ways that transcend the limits of logical understanding.

Clearly, this is not where we find ourselves today. Instead, we are surrounded by ugliness, hate, anger, division, degradation, and violence, all laid bare for us to witness. What began as a noble fight for equal rights and freedom of expression has devolved into a chaotic race to outdo one another in absurdity, vulgarity, and the grotesque. Absurd ideological Falsehoods are now paraded as Truths, and words once clear in their meaning have been weaponized, creating a linguistic minefield of confusion. This is textbook Chaos. Yet, in the grand scheme of things, it is no cause for despair—for we know that the seed of Order is quietly waiting to sprout when the molten eruption of Chaos has run its course.

Now, it's time to remove the bandage and confront the confusion—the festering wound at the heart of Western civilization.

At the heart of our collective chaos lies a profound spiritual crisis. Over the millennia and with striking acceleration since the advent of the industrial age and the rise of capitalism as the dominant global socio-economic system, humanity has lost its way. We have strayed far from the Grand Architecture of Creation, defaulting instead to the worship of a false prophet: the Religion of Money. In this modern gospel of unbridled capitalism, anything that cannot be quantified in monetary terms and cashed out at the Altar of Money has been systematically debased, dismissed, or outright ignored. Ethical values such as honesty, integrity, equity, justice, compassion, and solidarity have steadily eroded, while greed, exploitation, abuse of power, an insatiable hunger for material wealth, and unrestrained consumerism have become widely accepted as the "normal" way of modern life. In the process, exalted human qualities—Love, Truth, Honor, Nobility, Kindness, Generosity, and Respect for human dignity, to name a few—have been readily sacrificed for the abstractions venerated in the Religion of Money: power, fame, fortune, and applause.

Like a festering wound, this spiritual crisis has infected every corner of human society. The Religion of Money, with its transactional worldview, reduces all value to what can be bought, sold, or monetized. As a result, anything that defies commodification—be it the natural world, the sanctity of relationships, or the intrinsic dignity of the human spirit—is systematically undervalued, exploited, or outright disregarded. Even the arts, once a celebration of creativity and the divine spark within, have largely succumbed to commercial interests, judged not by their beauty or truth but by their profitability. Politics, education, healthcare, and even spiritual practices—especially in the form of organized religion, which have amassed immense wealth and often revel in opulence—have not escaped this corruption. They, too, are often molded to serve the interests of profit rather than their higher, nobler purposes.

This debasement of values has left humanity adrift in a sea of confusion, blind to the deeper meaning of existence. The imbalance between the material and spiritual realms has created a void—a hollow center where the Soul longs for nourishment. Yet, instead of filling this void with Truth, Love, Meaning, and Purpose, society continues to double down on material pursuits, mistaking them for the answers to its existential questions. This misplaced worship at the Altar of Money has plunged humanity into a profound disconnection—from itself, from others, and from the Grand Architecture of Creation.

Perhaps no greater microcosm of this spiritual and moral decay exists than Las Vegas, the epitome of glamour and glitter masking humanity's descent into its lower nature. Beneath its dazzling lights lies a celebration of escapism: a world fueled by alcohol, gambling, shopping, prostitution, debauchery, and gluttony. It is a shrine to excess, a perfect symbol of how far humanity has strayed from its higher purpose.

This spiritual crisis extends far beyond materialism. It manifests in the pervasive absence of meaning, purpose, and connection to something greater than ourselves. Devoid of a sense of higher purpose, countless individuals wander through life aimlessly, their souls aching for fulfillment yet perpetually seeking it in places that can never truly satisfy: alcohol, opioids, prescription drugs, gambling, shopping, pornography, and countless other distractions. The relentless pursuit of material success, status, pleasure, and sensory indulgences has become the default escape from existential despair. Yet, these pursuits offer only fleeting gratification—a shallow high that inevitably leaves behind a deeper void.

As a result, humanity faces an epidemic of spiritual emptiness. Depression, anxiety, addiction, and isolation have become the defining afflictions of modern life—symptoms of a society that has severed its connection to the sacred. We fill our calendars with distractions, our homes with possessions and endless disposables, and our minds with relentless noise, yet the quiet yearning for meaning persists. We have forgotten that our lives are threads woven into a greater cosmic tapestry. Without this connection, we drift aimlessly, like leaves on the wind, vulnerable to every gust of Chaos. Perhaps most tragic of all is how human despair, chronic illness, and overall brokenness are viewed not as crises to be resolved but as profit opportunities by the very system that created them.

This crisis isn't merely individual—it's collective. The absence of a shared higher purpose has left humanity fractured and divided; a civilization obsessed with consumption yet bereft of unity. Endless wars, savage bloodshed, and violence among peoples and nations are not only tolerated but systematically perpetuated, treated as profit centers for the vast military-industrial complex. This complex has no qualms about selling the tools of destruction and bloodshed for monetary gain. Nations exploit one another financially and economically, communities buckle under the weight of inequality, and relationships disintegrate into the haze of self-interest. We live in a world adrift, where GDP growth is held up as the ultimate measure of progress while the world itself sinks deeper into spiritual impoverishment and starvation. The Soul's hunger for Truth is drowned out by the unrelenting din of material ambition—a painful reminder that humanity, at large, is deeply and tragically lost.

That's the big picture. But now, let's shift our focus from the macro perspective and highlight some of the societal and cultural distortions that have emerged from this spiritual crisis. In these distortions, we find clear and troubling evidence of humanity being adrift—lost in a sea of confusion, disconnection, and despair.

About 1 in 17,000 people worldwide are affected by albinism. While rare, it is not unusual—this congenital absence of melanin is found in humans, animals, and even plants. Individuals with albinism face unique challenges, such as heightened sensitivity to sunlight and limitations in how they navigate life compared to others. Although they may encounter societal misunderstanding or ostracization, most reasonable people do not view them as freaks, less-than, or somehow inferior. Their inalienable rights as human beings are not in question—they were simply born this way, and that is their fate in this lifetime. So it goes with autism, the deaf or blind, people suffering from quadriplegia, and many others who live with rare conditions—whether the result of a genetic mutation or other factors—that are uncommon yet entirely natural parts of the human experience.

The entire subsection of the population that identifies as LGBTQ is no different. At approximately 7% of the population, they remain somewhat rare but are far from unusual. Homosexuality and bisexuality—which together make up roughly half of this group—have existed as natural facets of humanity since antiquity. Transgender individuals, at approximately 0.6% of the population, can be considered unequivocally rare, yet—once again—not unusual. In civilizations such as ancient Egypt, Greece, and the Roman Empire, homosexuality and bisexuality were not only accepted as a fact of life but were often celebrated as integral parts of society.

This phenomenon is not unique to humans. Scientists have observed same-sex sexual interactions in over 1,500 species across the animal kingdom, underscoring that these expressions of identity and behavior are simply part of Nature in its endless diversity. Whether in humans or wildlife, these variations are part of the vast, intricate tapestry of life—a reminder of the intelligence and creativity inherent in the Grand Architecture of Creation.

Nothing but clarity has emerged so far. Clearly, there should be no doubt or confusion that everyone within the LGBTQ community possesses the same inalienable rights as any other human being. They should be free to express themselves authentically, enjoy freedom of thought, and pursue happiness without obstruction or discrimination. They deserve our love, respect, and the assurance that they are welcomed as integral members of the human family. More than that, they should be enabled to thrive and prosper, unencumbered by prejudice or barriers imposed by outdated societal norms.

However, much like the case of albinism, being somewhat rare yet not unusual affords them no special rights or privileges to encroach upon the inalienable rights of others. We are either all free or none of us are truly free. You are entitled to your pronouns, ideas, ideologies, preferences, customs, and even costumes—but compelling others to conform to or adapt to your worldview is as egregious an assault on their inalienable rights as it would be if the roles were reversed.

Subjectively dismissing fundamental mammalian biology and imposing a scientifically baseless doctrine onto others is a textbook example of narcissism. The world owes you love and respect—nothing more. Likewise, you owe the world your love and respect—nothing less. This mutual recognition of rights and boundaries forms the cornerstone of a harmonious and equitable society. And truthfully, in a society anchored in Natural law and the spiritual principles that govern all of Creation, this would be self-evident.

Yes, the Truth can be a bitter tonic.

But dwelling in confusion serves no one. Clarity comes from the bitter tonic of Truth, even if it stings a little at first. So, let us honor this: you do you, and I will do me. I am in no way deny-ing that you are an integral part of the Grand Architecture of all Creation. We each possess undeniable, inalienable rights—equal to everyone else's without exception—and I, for one, would gladly defend those rights for anyone.

At the same time, it's important to clear away the confusion that has taken root. Each of us is unique in countless ways—a one-of-a-kind expression of the Divine. Some of us may fall on the far reaches of the bell curve, but that is merely a statistical observation, not a value judgment. This uniqueness in every individual is something to celebrate—a reminder that we each carry our own singular imprint of the Divine. Yet, while our individuality is worthy of recognition and respect, none of us are entitled to special privileges. When such privileges are claimed, they inevitably lead to imbalance and disharmony. As George Orwell so poignantly warned in *Animal Farm*, when "all animals are equal, but some animals are more equal than others" becomes embedded in the collective psyche or enshrined in the laws and systems of a civilization, it sets the stage for inevitable Chaos, conflict, and degradation.

Why? Because such an approach is neither coherent nor in alignment with the Grand Architecture of all Creation.

We must abide by the immutable laws that govern this Universe—it's as simple as that. Among these laws are the Masculine and Feminine Principles, which are not tied to gender, identity, or personal preferences. These principles are energetic Archetypes with distinct and unique attributes that transcend societal constructs and have nothing to do with how one identifies or what occurs in one's personal life. This book seeks to lay bare the Masculine Principles as they relate to and apply to biological males who are Masculine-dominant in their constitution. The sexual preference of these biological males is irrelevant to the exploration of these principles.

That said, albeit much rarer, there are also biological males who are Feminine-dominant in their constitution. These individuals may naturally exhibit qualities that society perceives as more feminine, but this does not necessarily mean they are gay, although they might be. While this book is not specifically written for those biological males who are Feminine-dominant, it still contains wisdom that may illuminate and inspire deeper understanding. For these individuals, this exploration can offer valuable insights into relating to Masculine-dominant males and understanding the dynamics of the principles presented here.

It's important to note that each man and woman, regardless of sexual preferences or gender identity, carries both the Masculine and Feminine Principles within the composition of their human avatar chosen for this lifetime. For the Masculine-dominant man, the Masculine archetype will naturally lead, just as the Feminine archetype will lead for the Feminine-dominant woman.

As we attain a certain level of spiritual mastery and maturity, we become "fully integrated." For the Masculine-dominant man, this integration means he embodies the exalted Masculine archetype while also having fully integrated—and therefore accessible to him—the exalted qualities of the Feminine archetype. This holistic integration is the hallmark of true spiritual evolution, where one's dominant energies are harmonized with their complementary aspects, allowing for a fuller, more balanced expression of the Divine within. Please note the sequel to this book—titled *Omega Sattva*—is centered around the rite of passage of becoming fully integrated and rising into the Christos archetype, or what Plato referred to as the *Philosopher-King* in his seminal work: the Republic.

For transgender individuals who identify as male and are Masculine-dominant, this book will likely serve you well. Masculinity is an energy field with its own distinct frequency signature, and to the extent that your Masculine-dominance is innate and not a construct of the Mind, this energy field operates independently of your biology. The principles explored here are rooted in universal Truths that transcend physical form, offering guidance for anyone aligned with the Masculine archetype in their essence.

This brings us to the Feminine, embodied most quintessentially by biological Feminine-dominant women as a fractal expression of the Divine. The Feminine Principle is but one aspect of this Divine expression, with the Masculine Principle as its complementary counterpart. The Masculine Principle is divinely entangled with the Feminine, their interplay inseparable, as beautifully visualized in the Yin-Yang symbol (the "Taijitu"). While we can study, analyze, and even dissect each principle individually, their true context lies in the harmonious divine union between them. Neither is complete or whole without the other. Together, they form an inseparable pair at the very core of the Grand Architecture of All Creation—equal in worth, yet vastly different in nature and essence.

Hence, we must now briefly examine the confusion created by the school of thought commonly referred to as modern-day feminism. At its core, the ideological foundation of modern-day feminism rests on a fundamental misunderstanding. This misunderstanding lies in the conflation of gender or biological sex with Femininity, which is an energy field possessing its own distinct frequency signature. Femininity, as an energetic principle, has a unique nature and distinct essence that is vastly different from Masculinity.

In the simplest terms, men and women are not wired the same. For clarity, when I speak of men and women from this point forward, I am referring to Masculine-dominant men and Feminine-dominant women, as they make up the overwhelming majority—roughly 90%—of all men and women, respectively. While there are individuals who do not fit this mold at the far reaches of the bell curve—some of whom I have already highlighted—these individuals, much like "Albinos," are not representative of the general population. Similarly, they are not representative of the Grand Architecture of all Creation.

This is not to say they are not part of Creation or that their existence is not valuable or any less meaningful or worthy. Nature expresses rarities, anomalies, irregularities, and abnormalities across all life forms with remarkable abundance and consistency, yet we can only recognize this because Nature overwhelmingly expresses itself in well-defined genetically coded patterns. So, this is how we know all the beautiful exceptions are simply not reflective of the broader patterns by which the totality of Creation functions and operates. This distinction is important because facts, even when uncomfortable or potentially offensive, bring us to clarity. Nature, governed by immutable laws, is indifferent to how we feel about her Truths. Ideas of what is offensive or inoffensive are psychological constructs—thoughts that are not inherently real, even if they appear real to us.

That said, while these constructs may not be real in the ultimate sense, the confusion they create can be as real and impactful as a heart attack when they stand in conflict with the immutable laws that govern all of Creation.

Modern-day feminism is built on the premise that men and women are the same—a deeply entrenched Falsehood that underpins much of its ideology. The reality is that men and women are not the same. Our biology is entirely different, and our dominant energies are fundamentally distinct. We are wired differently, down to our very physiology.

The female body, for instance, is far more complex than the male body due to its extraordinary capability to create life. This requires a significantly more advanced biological system compared to the male's far simpler role in procreation, which is to produce a dosage of sperm that barely fills a thimble. Additionally, men and women are governed by distinctly different dominant hormones—estrogen for women and testosterone for men.

When a woman's body experiences an estrogen deficit and a testosterone surplus, it disrupts her reproductive system, eventually leading to imbalance and a breakdown of homeostasis. The same happens to men in reverse when their testosterone levels drop and estrogen becomes dominant. These differences are not just scientific observations but fundamental Truths about human biology. This isn't rocket science—it's Nature operating as it was designed, and the Masculine archetype is simply not the same as the Feminine archetype.

Governed by our dominant energy, the emotional worlds of men and women are vastly different in both their makeup and how they function. The same applies to the mental plane. These differences are not new revelations—we all know this intuitively. Anyone who has interacted with or related to the opposite sex has experienced these distinctions firsthand. They are an inherent part of how we navigate the world as complementary expressions of the Masculine and Feminine Principles. And once again, none of this implies or suggests that one is better or more capable than the other. How we're fundamentally wired is not a reflection of our innate IQ, acumen, abilities, capabilities, gifts, talents, or superpowers, as these all vary widely between individuals regardless of gender.

Creating sameness or neutrality between these two opposite sexes is both ill-advised and counterproductive. In such a scenario, both men and women ultimately lose.

The historical confusion—and what feminism has revolted against—is the deeply flawed notion that men and women are not of equal worth or value. The Truth is, men and women are unequivocally equal in worth and value; they are simply different. And being different does not mean the playing field should not be level. Unfortunately, the playing field has been anything but level throughout history.

It's indisputable that women have been oppressed for the better part of humanity's history, suppressed, abused, devalued, belittled, ostracized, discriminated against, persecuted—and the list of atrocities committed against women by men could fill volumes. It wasn't that long ago that women were drowned, burned, or tortured based on nothing more than superstition. Even today, in certain parts of the world, girls and women endure horrific practices such as genital mutilation or are stoned to death in the name of preserving so-called family "honor." These injustices are stark reminders of the imbalance and harm caused when the inherent equality and dignity of women are not recognized or upheld.

The Truth can often be a bitter tonic. Men have committed these atrocities against women, and their revolt is entirely understandable. The ancestral wounds inflicted by men run deep—deeper than the Mariana Trench.

Still, sameness is not the answer.

Women are every bit as capable and intelligent as any man, and every woman who desires to build an empire, become a mogul or titan, excel in athletics, or climb the corporate ladder should be given the same opportunity as any man to do the same. Perfect clarity right there. And let's also be clear: this is not yet her total reality. Men have more work to do to address the imbalance in a system that was designed, built, and operated predominantly by men, for men, and to the advantage of men. While progress has been made, the work is not yet fully done.

That said, the energy that drives and fuels such ambitions in women is their Masculine energy, not their Feminine energy. By and large, women who naturally pursue and gravitate toward these paths tend to be Masculine-dominant or have a strong Masculine energy within their overall human design and composition. And there is absolutely nothing wrong with that—it is their prerogative and inalienable right to choose their own path.

However, it's worth noting that Masculine-dominant women—many of whom are the driving force behind modern feminism—may find that Masculine-dominant men are magnetically drawn to Feminine-dominant women (and vice versa). Opposites attract; this is not merely a preference but a principle rooted in the laws of physics. Everything is energetic in nature, and the immutable laws of Creation govern this dynamic. The complementary interplay of energies is the foundation of attraction and harmonic balance.

We can argue against and oppose these immutable laws, spending a lifetime dwelling in confusion. Or, we can seek to understand and recognize these laws, align with them, and come into coherence with the natural order. In doing so, we step into total clarity. This is a choice each of us is free to make.

A Feminine-dominant woman will naturally desire to be with a Masculine-dominant man, and the reverse is equally true. She may choose to express her innate talents in her work, even flourish professionally, but her Feminine essence will still naturally and harmoniously seek to be led by the Masculine essence of her man. Her essence yearns for his Masculine energy to create a container of safety, protection, and provision that spans the physical, emotional, intellectual, and spiritual realms.

If he cannot provide this—if he lacks the love, care, and devotion necessary for her to trust him—she cannot fully surrender to his lead, and the relationship will inevitably falter. Once again, he must continuously earn her love and respect; there are no shortcuts or freebies for him. His ability to energetically hold this space for her is the foundation upon which trust, surrender, and harmony are built.

Incidentally, within this harmonious union, her innate and exquisite Feminine qualities and attributes sustain, inspire, and enrich him in profoundly different yet equally meaningful ways. It is this sacred interplay between the Masculine and Feminine that creates the dynamic balance and mutual nourishment upon which their relationship thrives.

A union of sameness is bound to feel lacking for both individuals. In contrast, a union of the Masculine and Feminine Principles—embodied by a man and woman coming together in a sacred union—represents the completion of the divine Source Consciousness. They complement one another, each becoming more whole and more complete, rising to greater heights together than they ever could alone. This is sheer Divine poetry. Yet, in today's world, this timeless universal Truth is often dismissed as antiquated nonsense.

There is an important nuance to highlight regarding this dynamic. First, in general terms, Masculine-dominance will naturally seek and be attracted to its energetic counterpart in Feminine-dominance, and vice versa. This is the concept of energetic matching. Second, while I reference this sacred union as being embodied by a man and woman, these exact energetic principles also apply to LGBTQ unions (which are equally sacred and hence worthy of all legal privileges afforded by marriage), where one partner expresses a more Masculine-dominant energy and the other a more Feminine-dominant energy. The interplay of these energies transcends gender or sexual orientation and operates at the level of universal principles.

At the heart of the confusion underlying feminist ideology is the belief that a woman in a traditional role—such as being a devoted mother and wife—is somehow marginalized or diminished. Because these roles do not traditionally produce a paycheck, the assumption is often that she must, therefore, be taken advantage of. This is a clear example of how the Religion of Money has grossly distorted perceptions, reducing value to only what can be expressed in monetary terms and cashed out at the Altar of Money. Motherhood and being a wife are devalued in the framework of this belief system simply because they do not come with a paycheck. Yet, motherhood, arguably, might be the most important, beautiful, and valuable role in all of society.

And what if this is exactly the role that she desires for herself? What if she derives immense value, fulfillment, and purpose from being a devoted mother and homemaker in a loving union where she feels fully seen, heard, and cherished? What if *Being* his wife is deeply meaningful to her, and their partnership works beautifully for both of them?

What if, in their chosen way of organizing and nurturing their union, they each find purpose, fulfillment, and happiness? Who is to say that their union is any less valuable or meaningful simply because it does not conform to modern societal expectations or because there is nothing for her to cash out at the Altar of Money?

Contrary to popular feminist belief, this is what many—if not most—naturally Feminine-dominant women aspire to and desire when they are liberated from the doctrines of the Religion of Money. For clarity, this refers to the majority of women since the majority is Feminine-dominant, and while they have varying degrees of aspirations of some form of professional fulfillment, most naturally aspire to have the time and freedom from suffocating professional pressures and expectations to be mothers and care for their families. However, societal programming and the modern-day feminist agenda have not only encouraged but pushed women onto a treadmill of grinding it out in careers, chasing trophies, and pursuing financial independence as a measure of their "true worth." This narrative suggests that by becoming financially independent, a woman can finally assert her independence from men.

The confusion lies in the belief that her "true worth" is tied to financial independence or professional accomplishments. Her worth was never about finances or career achievements, and neither was his. Her dependence on men was not the real issue either. The deeper wound—an ancestral wound—was inflicted by a male-oriented, male-dominated society that oppressed, devalued, and abused women for millennia. It was this systemic devaluation that made her feel unequal in worth and value, leaving a legacy of pain and confusion in its wake, which she believed could only be corrected by joining men in pursuing meaning in abstractions such as wealth, fame, fortune, and applause that can be cashed out at the Altar of Money.

So, she had an axe to grind and became determined to prove her "worth" vis-à-vis men the moment she was given the smallest chance to do so. The confusion in all of this is that her "worth" was never tied to the Finite Games of chasing trophies that men play. As this book will explore in depth, even his true "worth" is not derived from those pursuits—he's been in fact pathologically and anthropologically confused about this from the beginning of time. Her attempt to claim her "worth" by stepping into the same misguided games men play only perpetuates and deepens this self-perpetuating cycle of Mankind's utter confusion about the true purpose of Life.

This confusion has taken root so deeply that it has contributed to the profound spiritual crisis humanity faces today—a crisis that risks extinguishing the flickering pilot light of soulfulness in exchange for a soulless existence as a cog in the machinery of a synthetic transhumanist surveillance state, all premised on the doctrines of the Religion of Money.

The Truth is, her true "worth" simply is, just as his is. She is inherently worthy simply by *Being* her true self, in whichever way she chooses to express that. Perhaps her path leads her to a career or to winning Olympic gold. Maybe it's becoming a devoted mother or volunteering with the Peace Corps in Africa. Whatever her path, her worth remains constant, untouched by the metrics of societal expectations or the external trophies the world may chase. Her worth is intrinsic, immutable, and beyond the reach of any finite game.

Money, success, trophies, status, accolades, achievements—none of these ever define anyone's worth. They are an erroneous yardstick, a flawed measure of value. What you do is ultimately irrelevant; your true worth lies in who you are *Being* in the ever-present Now.

Only with perfect clarity on the modern-day context—a world shaped by humanity functioning and operating as a male-oriented and male-dominated society—can we fully understand how vitally important it is for men, as a collective, to rise into the exalted Masculine archetype. Let there be no confusion: the Religion of Money and its countless reflections in the state of the world today are creations born from a spiritually void collective Masculine that has descended into its lower nature. It is a Masculine that has lost touch with its exalted archetype, forgotten its true essence, and abandoned its sacred role in the greater tapestry of Creation here in the earthly realm.

The Masculine archetype, then, is the medicine. The restoration of the Feminine archetype to its full luminescence, genius, and rightful place alongside the Masculine cannot fully occur without the Masculine archetype first being restored. Only when the collective Masculine, as embodied by mortal men, rises into its exalted expression can the harmony and balance of Creation be reestablished.

The Masculine must lead. The sperm fertilizes the egg, not the other way around. Similarly, the resurrection of the Masculine archetype can only be achieved by men rising into their exalted Masculine essence.

Yet, he must earn his Masculine stripes, so to speak. He must not only do the spiritual attunement work but also express this spiritual work into the material realm with absolute accountability and unwavering responsibility. It is his sacred duty to devote his entire *Being* to carving his David out of the marble, removing all that is excess and unnecessary until only his true essence remains.

The rest of this book serves as a field guide for him—a roadmap to rise into the Masculine archetype and reclaim his Divine essence so he might become what the Creator and Most High envisioned him to be—a fully realized *Alpha Virtus*.

The exalted Masculine archetype is *the* medicine. Let's get to work.

Once you see, you cannot unsee.

INITIATION

RGUABLY, A MAN'S ENTIRE LIFE IS ONE NEVER-ending initiation. But since that's not a particularly helpful vantage point to initiate men into what initiation truly is, we'll strip it back a few layers.

A man's initiation into manhood comes through challenges—an endless barrage of trials and tribulations that will either forge his mettle or see him succumb to the pressures, degrading into a soft and emasculated man. Girls, by contrast, are initiated into womanhood by Nature. When she first menstruates, she becomes a woman as far as Nature is concerned. In that sense, she has no real choice in the matter.

Men, however, must make the choice—time and again.

When a man enters trade school to learn carpentry, mechanics, plumbing, or electrical work, he becomes an Initiate—what we commonly call an apprentice. He may be a complete novice in his chosen trade, but simply stepping into trade school makes him an Initiate. His sole purpose is to gain mastery through devotion to what he's being initiated into. If it's carpentry, his goal is to become a master carpenter, which he achieves by learning skills and techniques from mentors and working tirelessly on his craft.

The path of an Initiate is filled with countless challenges. It demands perseverance, resilience, grit, tenacity, patience, ingenuity, strength, courage, and unwavering commitment. It is a gauntlet that tests his mindset and mettle under intense pressure, forging him into something stronger, better, and more enduring.

If, at any point, he cracks and cannot find a way to rise again, he loses his Soul. His trajectory in life is stunted. He will no longer reach his full potential in this lifetime. Instead, he will live a life dominated and ruled by others. His choices and opportunities will narrow, and this limitation extends even to his relationships—women intuitively sense a man who has lost his Soul. He's not soulless, but he is bankrupt, and a bankrupt Soul is left with life's breadcrumbs.

He may still function outwardly: hold a job, provide for a family, and embody the usual trappings of life. But his expression will be muted. He will conform to the system and submit his will to others—possibly even to his wife. Something inside of him has already died.

This is the "dead man walking"—the man who was destroyed by life and has surrendered to defeat.

You see, men will face destruction—it's inevitable. Over the course of his life, a man will be destroyed time and again. He will endure heartbreak, lose the championship match, get rejected by his crush, lose his job, or watch a business or his finances collapse. He will bury loved ones, be betrayed by friends or partners, and likely experience infidelity, relationship crises, or divorce. Whatever it may be, he will face it—and it will destroy him.

But all of this destruction exists in the Outer World. As long as a man gets back up, he cannot be defeated. Defeat resides solely in his Inner World—the very sanctuary of his Soul.

Destruction in the Outer World may be inevitable, but defeat is not. He is only truly defeated when he chooses not to rise again.

This is his journey in life: to be destroyed time and again but never to be defeated. As the shepherd and guardian of his Soul, his ultimate task is to ensure that no matter what happens in the Outer World, he does not succumb to defeat in his Inner World. Everything is at stake here.

Then there are the soulless men. Our world is full of them, spanning across all walks of life. These men have capitulated to their lower nature, choosing not to rise above it. They are not so much defeated as they are confused, mistaking the Finite Games men play in the Outer World for the true purpose of life.

They ignore—or lack the courage to step into—the Infinite Game that the Spirit plays, the one true game encompassing all others.

By definition, all Finite Games are played within the framework of the Infinite Game. Yet, these men remain stuck in the minor leagues, either knowingly or unknowingly. Many appear highly successful in the Outer World—they may be wealthy, powerful, and influential, surrounded by praise and admiration. But a closer look often reveals a life steeped in gluttony, debauchery, emptiness, and frequently a messy trail of fraud, malfeasance, lies, and harm inflicted on others.

Not all, but most of our politicians and titans of industry fall into this category. Once you develop the discernment to see it, their lives become pitiful sights, empty shells propped up by the illusions and abstract trappings of the Outer World.

But do not despair, for there is always a way out. Any man—whether defeated or soulless—has the option to freely choose to become an Initiate of the one Infinite Game. This book may help him see that this is the only path to escape the quicksand of defeat and soullessness.

The good news is that becoming an Initiate of the Infinite Game does not require anything from the Outer World. A man can be completely broke, broken, or destitute and still be eligible to step onto this path at any time.

The Infinite Game plays out entirely in the Inner World, but its impact will unmistakably manifest in the Outer World. Through this journey, a man will discover his true Power—a

Power so immutable and profound that he will wonder how it had been lying dormant within him for so long.

But to harness this Power, a man must first freely choose to become an Initiate. He must face the excruciating trials and tribulations that come with purifying himself. He must overcome and master his lower nature, gaining full mastery over his Masculine essence through complete embodiment.

This path is not easy. The weak will falter, for it will test and stretch the Initiate to the very limits of his capacities. Yet, it is through this crucible that a man forges his mettle. Everything must be earned, including and especially the respect of the Creator and Most High.

This book will tell you how. But if you have no intention of becoming an Initiate, there is no need to read further. I have no bone in that fight; that is between you and your Soul. My role is merely to illuminate the path for those who are ready to walk it.

Once you see, you cannot unsee.

ALPHA

THE MYTH AND THE TRUTH ABOUT ALPHA

THE TERM ALPHA HAS BEEN HIJACKED. IN MODERN culture, it conjures an image of the dominant male (or possibly female)—commanding, powerful, leading the pack through sheer force of will. The Alpha is framed as the pinnacle of masculinity, at the top of the hierarchy, and the man all others follow.

But this portrayal is superficial and incomplete—a pop-culture fabrication that reduces masculinity to status, dominance, and power struggles. The Alpha we're concerned with originates within the Alpha & Omega, an expression of a higher Truth which has a far deeper meaning and significance than any social archetype or a position in a hierarchy—Alpha then symbolizes an origin point, a beginning, an initiation.

Alpha is the starting point of mastery—not its final destination.

Hence, the title *Alpha Virtus* does not refer to some socio-sexual status, hierarchical position in society, or even a biologically hard-wired natural dominance. Rather, it speaks to the first step of the journey—the initiation into an exalted state of *Being*. It is the threshold every man must cross if he is to rise into his highest expression. It is the call to awaken, to refine, to embody Virtus—the essence of masculine virtue.

In this chapter, we will strip away the illusions surrounding the Alpha archetype—the myths, the misconceptions, and the cultural noise while also highlighting what's useful—and uncover what it truly means to embody the first step toward sovereignty, mastery, and alignment with deeper Truths of Life itself.

ALPHA & OMEGA
The Masculine and Feminine Principle

Beyond its reference to the beginning and the end, Alpha & Omega also represents something far more fundamental: the interplay of the exalted Masculine and the exalted Feminine— the two primordial forces that shape all of creation.

Alpha is the Masculine Principle—structure, will, initiation, discipline, and direction. It is the force that carves pathways, builds order, and brings form to the formless. It is the riverbank that gives shape to the rushing waters of Life, the mountain that stands unmoved in the face of the storm.

Omega is the Feminine Principle—fluidity, receptivity, intuition, and surrender to the great unfolding. It is the vast ocean, deep and mysterious, flowing with the intelligence of Life itself. It is the void from which all things emerge, the creative force that nourishes, expands, and dissolves.

These two forces are not opposites in conflict; they are complements in harmony. The exalted Masculine is not rigid control, nor is the exalted Feminine passive chaos. Together, they dance— structure and flow, action and grace, movement and stillness.

The unawakened man, trapped in his unconscious programming, often finds himself disconnected from this sacred union. He either clings to a distorted Masculinity—one of force, suppression, and domination—or he rejects it altogether, becoming untethered, lacking the spine to stand in his own sovereignty.

But the man walking the path of true Alpha embodiment understands this sacred interplay. He does not seek to overpower the Feminine, nor does he deny its presence within himself. Instead, he honors, integrates, and governs it wisely—within himself first and in his Outer World second.

This is why *Alpha Virtus* is only the initiation. It is the first step—a man rising into his sovereign Masculine, building the foundation upon which all else rests. But without its counterpart, it remains incomplete.

Upon initiation, this path will continue with *Omega Sattva*— the second book in this series—the completion of this sacred journey. It is where the sovereign Masculine integrates the exalted Feminine within, and in the process, transcends his earthly archetype to become a fully realized Christos—what the ancient Greeks referred to as a mortal God or the *Philosopher-King*, a pure reflection of the Godhead.

These are the esoteric wisdom teachings of the ancient mystery schools, which taught that true ascension required the merging of Alpha & Omega, Christos and Sophia, Masculine and Feminine, Wisdom and Love.

To walk the path of Alpha is to initiate.

To walk the path of Omega is to transcend.

And only through this union does a man reach the highest octave of his *Being*.

But before a man is ready to embark on his journey of Omega transcendence, he must first walk the path of his Alpha initiation.

So, let's focus on the task at hand: mastering Alpha.

THE MISCONCEPTION OF THE ALPHA

The modern world has built a mythology around the Alpha archetype—a caricature rather than a reality. In mainstream narratives, the Alpha male is the apex predator, the dominant force, the man who bends the world to his will through sheer strength, charisma, or cunning. He is the leader of men, the conqueror of women, the embodiment of control.

This is the fiction. The truth is something else entirely.

Much of the mythology surrounding the Alpha male is rooted in quackery social pseudo-science—oversimplified dominance hierarchies borrowed from flawed animal studies, then misapplied to human behavior. The infamous "Alpha wolf" model, for instance, was based on observations of captive wolves forced into unnatural social conditions. In the wild, however, wolf packs operate as family units, with leadership based on wisdom, cooperation, and care rather than brute force.

The same principle applies to men: Leadership and sovereignty are not determined by competition, aggression, or dominance but by alignment with deeper Truths with integrity through inner strength.

Yet, even beyond the pseudo-scientific distortions, there is an undeniable truth: Some men are born with stronger innate Alpha traits—natural confidence, drive, or a capacity to lead. However, when these traits are expressed through the shadows of the unrefined Masculine, the Alpha man quickly becomes a destructive force. A man who has not mastered himself will inevitably seek to dominate and manipulate others to compensate for his own lack of self-governance.

An uninitiated Alpha, lacking wisdom and virtue, becomes a tyrant—narcissistic, impulsive, and reckless. His natural strength becomes a weapon against the world rather than a foundation for stewardship. His leadership turns into manipulation, his charisma into deceit, his ambition into self-serving conquest. Left unchecked, this unrefined Alpha does not build—he consumes and exploits.

This is why the first step toward true Alpha embodiment is self-governance.

The true Alpha man is not merely born—he is forged through his virtues, his trials, and his ability to refine his innate strengths into something noble. Without this refinement, the Alpha man remains a force of chaos rather than a force of creation.

The path of mastery does not begin with control over others. It begins with sovereignty over oneself.

This is the true Alpha we are concerned with—not a social archetype, dominance strategy, or something we are either born with or not. The true Alpha is not an archetype but the first step toward an embodied, attuned, and exalted way of *Being*. The Alpha of Alpha & Omega. The beginning of the luminous path.

Now, let us strip away the illusions and examine the traits of the true Alpha—the one who walks the luminous path. The true Alpha does not merely take but builds; does not seek control but commands respect; does not react to life but governs himself with sovereignty before ever leading another. He is not an archetype to be imitated but an embodiment to be lived.

THE SOCIAL ARCHETYPES
A Functional Framework

If we strip away the myths and distortions surrounding the concept of Alpha, what remains is a broader set of archetypal patterns that describe different ways men engage with the world. While the dominance-based hierarchy has been popularized as the defining model of masculinity, the reality is far more complex.

The Alpha-Beta-Sigma-Delta-Gamma framework is often treated as a rigid ranking system, where men are either leaders (Alphas), followers (Betas), or outsiders (Sigmas). But this is an oversimplification. In truth, these archetypes are fluid expressions of masculine tendencies, not fixed roles a man is locked into for life.

A man may embody different aspects of these archetypes in different situations. He may operate as a Beta in one context— loyal, dependable, and following the leadership of someone he respects—but then exhibit Sigma-like independence when pursuing a passion or a deeply personal goal. He may embrace Alpha-level responsibility in his career but adopt a more Delta-like humility in areas where he prefers to stay in the background.

The key distinction is this: Hierarchy is not destiny.

Men are not bound to a predetermined rank in some social pecking order. These archetypes simply describe behavioral tendencies, not fixed identities. What distinguishes a man who is truly sovereign from a man who is bound by external validation is not whether he is "Alpha" or "Sigma"—it is whether he is governing himself or being governed by his environment.

CULTURAL ALPHA VS. TRUE ALPHA

To further clarify this, let's distinguish between the cultural Alpha—the dominant male archetype popularized by media and pop psychology—and the true Alpha, the Initiate who is not defined by dominance over others but by mastery over himself.

The cultural Alpha:

- Defined by status, power, and social rank.
- Seeks to dominate others rather than govern himself.
- Measures success through external validation—accolades, wealth, or sexual conquests.
- Operates from competition, constantly seeking to prove his worth by comparing himself to others.
- Often leads through force, charisma, or manipulation rather than wisdom.
- His power is fragile—if he loses status, his sense of self crumbles.

The true Alpha:

- Defined by self-governance, responsibility, and inner mastery.
- Does not seek to control others—he controls himself.
- Measures success by who he is *Being* rather than what he has.
- Operates from inner alignment, not from external competition.
- Leads through integrity, wisdom, and personal example.
- His power is unshakable—because it does not depend on status or validation.

The cultural Alpha is an illusion built on fragile foundations. The true Alpha is the man on the path of Initiation, a way of *Being* that any man can choose to walk, regardless of his natural archetypal tendencies.

BEYOND THE HIERARCHY
Transcendence Over Rank

For the man walking the path of true mastery, the goal is not to move higher in a hierarchy—it is to step out of it altogether.

The dominance hierarchy is a game society teaches men to play from an early age. We are conditioned to compete, to measure ourselves against others, to derive our sense of worth from how we rank in comparison. This game keeps men locked in a cycle of external validation, always chasing the next proof of their superiority—more money, more women, more status.

But the true Alpha does not play this game.

Instead of competing within the hierarchy, he governs himself and builds his own Kingdom—one that is not measured by power over others but by his substance as a man and his ability to lead himself.

His measure of success is not how many men follow him but how unwavering he remains in his own truth.

The world will always try to pull a man into its fabricated hierarchies, convincing him that his worth must be proven rather than embodied. But the man who truly initiates into his highest expression understands:

The game worth winning most is the game within.

The only rank that matters is the one he holds within himself.

The only Kingdom worth creating is the one he builds through his own sovereignty.

This is the path ahead. A man does not need to be born an Alpha. He simply needs to decide if he's ready to start *Being* one.

THE SOVEREIGNTY OF THE TRUE ALPHA

A man does not become the true Alpha by seeking dominance, nor does he rise to his highest expression by following someone else's blueprint for power. He becomes the true Alpha by choosing sovereignty—by mastering himself rather than seeking to control the world around him.

Sovereignty is not about external power; it is about internal authority. The true Alpha does not need validation, permission, or approval. He does not chase status, nor does he rely on the opinions of others to determine his worth. He is unshakable because his foundation is built from within, not from the ever-changing tides of the external world.

This sovereignty is reflected in how he carries himself. He speaks when he has something meaningful to say, not to impress or to dominate. He moves with certainty, not arrogance. He makes decisions from clarity, not impulse. His presence is not forced—it simply is.

The sovereignty of the true Alpha is also reflected in his ability to stand alone. Many men fear solitude because they are dependent on external structures to define them. The true Alpha knows that aloneness is not loneliness—it is strength. His value is not determined by the size of his following but by the depth of his integrity. He walks his path with confidence, whether others walk beside him or not.

But sovereignty does not mean isolation. A truly sovereign man is capable of deep connection. This is because he does not approach relationships from need but from wholeness. He does not manipulate or control, nor does he seek to be completed by another. He chooses his relationships from a place of abundance, not scarcity.

Sovereignty also demands responsibility. The true Alpha owns his decisions, his actions, and his failures. He does not make excuses or seek to shift blame. When he missteps, he corrects course. When he falls, he rises again. This unwavering ownership of self is what makes him a man that others naturally trust, respect, and follow—not because he demands it but because his presence commands it.

Ultimately, sovereignty is the defining trait of the true Alpha. He is not a ruler over others—he is the undisputed governor of himself. And from this place, he does not need to try to be a leader. He simply is.

This is the difference between the cultural Alpha and the true Alpha.

One seeks control. The other embodies power.

One chases validation. The other is his own validation.

One plays the game. The other is the game.

And in that sovereignty, the true Alpha does not need to become anything.

He simply is.

Once you see, you cannot unsee.

VIRTUS

WE ARE AT THE DAWN OF A NEW ERA. THROUGH-out history, humanity has evolved from its primitive hunter-gatherer origins through a series of civilizations, each more advanced than the one that preceded it.

Civilizations rise, peak, and inevitably fall apart, dissolving into the pages of history. Whether it was Ancient Egypt, Greece, the Roman Empire, the Mayan civilization, or any other empire, the pattern remains the same.

What causes civilizations to collapse is rarely an external force, even when conquest delivers the final blow. The real downfall is erosion from within. Corruption and moral decay creep into the core of the power structure, and leaders often descend into despots, tyrants, or dictators. These figures embody the rot, reveling in grandiose opulence while exploiting the very people they are meant to lead. This inner corruption eats away at the integrity of the civilization, leaving it brittle and vulnerable to collapse.

This pattern of internal decay is no coincidence; it is a manifestation of a deeper spiritual crisis. When leaders and societies forsake higher principles in favor of greed, power, and indulgence, they disconnect from the natural order and the intelligence of Life itself. This disconnection leads to stagnation and decline—a violation of Nature's immutable laws, where everything must evolve and regenerate perpetually.

The final stages of a civilization's collapse are unmistakable. Entropy sets in, and Chaos begins to overtake Order. The fabric of society frays, hairline fractures spread, and the seams eventually rupture. Conflict, violence, power struggles, infighting, division, and rampant self-serving behavior among the elites become the norm. Leaders who were once trusted stewards of their civilizations become consumed by greed and self-interest, accelerating the descent into disorder.

This is the natural arc of stagnation and decay. Civilizations stop regenerating and lose alignment with the intelligence of Nature, which demands evolution and renewal.

If this sounds familiar, it's because we can clearly observe these signs in Western civilization today. The writing is on the wall: a collapse is coming, followed by a vacuum—a period of apparent disarray before rebirth begins.

This vacuum is not inherently good or bad; it is simply a transition. When Nature burns down a forest with wildfire, there is a period of stillness after the flames die down. But beneath the ashes lie seeds of new life, dormant yet ready to sprout. These seeds are the Order that emerges from Chaos, the green shoots of renewal waiting to regenerate.

To understand Nature is to understand the intelligence of Life itself. To grasp the inner workings of Creation is to step into the role of an empowered Creator.

Humanity's story began with our earliest ancestors evolving into *Homo sapiens*, a process scientists estimate began roughly 550,000 to 750,000 years ago. While the history that predates this is not irrelevant, for our discussion, the period since the Renaissance is of greatest importance.

The Renaissance, spanning the 15th and 16th centuries, marked humanity's transition from the darkness of the Middle Ages into the era of modernity. It was a period of awakening and transformation that laid the foundation for the world we live in today.

This new era ushered in an explosion of scientific discoveries and technological advancements. Chemistry, astronomy, medicine, biology, and geology rapidly evolved due to their practical applications. Over time, humanity expanded its reach into fields like advanced mathematics, physics, quantum mechanics, and engineering. These breakthroughs gave rise to engines, railroads, factories, electricity, and, more recently, computers, software, the internet, and artificial intelligence. Humanity has been busy indeed.

But alongside this scientific revolution came a new economic system: capitalism. This system, initially designed to fund and accelerate innovation, began to exploit and monetize these advances. Fractional banking emerged when goldsmiths realized they could issue more IOUs than they had gold to back them. What began as a practical solution evolved into the global economic framework we live within today.

Over time, capitalism became more than just an economic system—it became humanity's predominant religion, giving rise to the Religion of Money. Nations began to measure their health and progress almost exclusively through Gross Domestic Product (GDP). Domestic policies revolved around GDP, wars were fought over it, and societies came to define success solely in economic terms.

Ironically, Simon Kuznets, the economist who developed GDP, cautioned that while it is a useful economic indicator, it is a poor measure of human well-being. Yet, somewhere along the way, this warning was ignored. The worth of a nation—and even the worth of an individual—became synonymous with economic output.

In short, *Homo Sapiens* evolved into *Homo Economicus*, adopting the value system decreed by the Religion of Money. This system systematically debases anything that cannot be expressed in monetary units and "cashed out" at the Altar of Money, reducing the vast richness of life to mere financial transactions.

Moreover, the ethos of Human Dignity, Integrity, Honor, Nobility, Compassion, Fairness, Justice, and even the Sanctity of Life itself all suffered erosion. Reverence for Nature and our planet was readily sacrificed at the Altar of Money in the pursuit of wealth, power, status, and accolades. This system birthed atrocities such as colonialism, the slave trade, corporate imperialism, and endless wars drenched in bloodshed, all fought over territory and resources.

As we explored earlier, everything is a fractal of a larger fractal. What holds true on a macro level also applies to the individual. Just as GDP is a poor measure of a nation's well-being, your personal "GDP" is a poor measure of your overall quality of life.

This truth is glaringly evident today. Humanity, as a collective, is wealthier and more prosperous than ever before in recorded history. Yet, the disparities in wealth are staggering, and even those who have hoarded the lion's share of prosperity are far from thriving. The symptoms of this imbalance are everywhere: obesity, chronic illness, pharmaceutical dependency, addiction, stress, anxiety, burnout, depression, divorce, and suicide. These afflictions have become so prevalent that we have collectively normalized them as part of modern life.

Meanwhile, humanity's relentless pursuit of economic growth has left the planet scarred. We have poisoned the soil, polluted the air and water, and ravaged ecosystems to the point where the biosphere teeters on the brink of ecological collapse. In this dire situation, humanity's latest imagined miracle cure is to engineer its way out of its predicament through artificial intelligence (AI or AGI). The prevailing hope is that technology and science will save the day, even as our unintelligent use of those same tools created many of these problems in the first place.

But here's the fundamental truth: the core problem cannot be solved with more technology or scientific advancements. Our technological and scientific capabilities have far outpaced our spiritual maturity. Without the wisdom and intelligence required to deploy these tools responsibly, they only serve to exacerbate the chaos. What humanity truly lacks is not better technology—it's a more developed spiritual pedigree, one that can guide us toward wiser, more harmonious solutions.

Every novice in systems engineering understands that when you design, integrate, and manage complex systems using the wrong indicators, you're bound to end up with a mess at best—or, more likely, a catastrophic collapse.

Humanity, along with its societies and the economies functioning within them, is a profoundly complex system. Yet, GDP—a rudimentary metric at best—has been used as the primary measure of these economies. These economies are nested within societies, which are themselves nested within humanity, which is nested within the intricate web of Nature on planet Earth, which is further nested within the Milky Way galaxy, and so on.

Imagine trying to fly a plane from New York to London using nothing but the tire pressure of the landing gear as your guide. It's an absurd notion, but it perfectly encapsulates the misguided way humanity has been navigating its trajectory.

This entire era of modernity is collapsing under its own weight. It has outlived its time and useful purpose, and with it, *Homo Economicus* has, for all intents and purposes, entered hospice care.

Hospice care doesn't mean immediate death; it is a process, a slow unraveling. *Homo Economicus* may linger for a while yet, giving every man alive today a choice: to continue frolicking along with the values and systems of *Homo Economicus* and continuing to kneel down at the Altar of Money or to prepare himself for what's coming next.

This book is not about clinging to the ways of the past. It is about preparing for the future. You won't find advice here on how to improve your personal GDP or conform to the crumbling systems of the Religion of Money that birthed *Homo Economicus*. Instead, this book is a guide to what's coming next—a new archetype for manhood and humanity that aligns with the era on the horizon.

When you embody the principles and virtues outlined in this book, you will no longer be preoccupied with improving your personal GDP. Your self-worth will no longer be measured by your net worth—a radical shift away from the value system of the Religion of Money.

This transformation begins in the Inner World. By embodying the virtues described in this book, you will become a man of true worth. And here's the beauty of it: the immutable laws of physics dictate that like-energy attracts like-energy. When you embody worth, you radiate value. When you radiate value, the Outer World will naturally compensate you in kind.

But this is not a passive process. The virtues must be embodied—they must become who you are, moment by moment, in everything you do. This work demands commitment and discipline, but it frees you from the need to chase external markers of success. Instead of obsessing over your personal GDP, you will discover that you have what you need and can procure what you want—not because of external metrics, but because you are aligned with the intelligence of Life itself.

Now, let's talk about *Virtus*.

The word *Virtus* means "virtues" in Latin. The Romans, paradoxical as they were, understood the significance of virtues as the foundation of the exalted Masculine archetype. They were both barbaric and visionary—a civilization that butchered entire populations and reveled in the savagery of gladiator games, yet also achieved incredible feats of architecture, engineering, and art. Their philosophical legacy, Stoicism, endures as a testament to their intellectual depth.

In many ways, the Romans sowed the seeds of the central idea espoused in this book: that *Virtus* represents the highest state of the Masculine archetype. While they often failed to fully embody this ideal or make it central to their civilization, they were onto something profound.

What's collapsing today is the era of *Homo Economicus*, and what will rise from the ashes is *Homo Virtus*. Beneath the current chaos, confusion, and entropy, the seeds of the next era have already been planted. The transition is inevitable, as Nature makes no mistakes. Humanity must evolve, rising to a higher level of consciousness to meet the challenges of the future.

At these higher levels of consciousness, humanity will gain access to higher intelligence. Solutions that seem impossible or imperceivable from the perspective of *Homo Economicus* will become self-evident to *Homo Virtus*.

As Albert Einstein famously said, "You cannot solve a problem from the same level of thinking that created it." Intelligence, in this context, is tied to consciousness. The only way forward is to elevate our collective consciousness, which will, in turn, unlock a higher octave of intelligence and clarity.

As humanity teeters on the brink of collapse, there is a misguided belief that artificial intelligence (AI) or artificial general intelligence (AGI) will be the savior of our predicament. The logic follows that technology and science, which created many of the challenges we face, can somehow engineer a way out of the mess.

But here's the fundamental flaw: our technological and scientific capabilities have outpaced our spiritual maturity. Without a foundation of wisdom, reverence for life, and alignment with the intelligence of Nature, these tools can only deepen the Chaos. Humanity doesn't suffer from a lack of technology—it suffers from a lack of spiritual intelligence, a deficiency in the inner understanding required to wield external Power responsibly.

AI itself is not inherently bad. In the hands of *Homo Virtus*, it has the potential to elevate humanity to unprecedented heights, bending the arc of civilization toward harmony, creativity, and abundance. But in the careless hands of *Homo Economicus*, AI could easily become a tool for dystopian control, fueling a soulless surveillance state.

Although we're playing with fire and humanity is facing a potential societal collapse or even extinction event, I steadfastly believe this dystopian trajectory will fortunately not fully mate-rialize—the current system will self-destruct before it can reach an ultimate cataclysmic end. But for this collapse to pave the way for renewal and rebirth of a new era, there must be a counter-weight: men willing to evolve and rise into *Homo Virtus*.

For humanity to bend the arc of its destiny in the right direc-tion, we need enough men to evolve into *Homo Virtus*. This is why this book is titled *Alpha Virtus* and not *Homo Virtus*. My aim is to enlist men—to provide them with a field guide to step into the exalted Masculine archetype and embody the virtues necessary to meet the challenges of this new era.

Let me be clear: this is not about exclusion or division. This book is for all men, regardless of background, identity, or circum-stance. You're a man. Choose how you want to live your life and express it fully. I am in the business of guiding Souls, teaching the intelligence of Life itself, and helping those who seek my help to curate their highest potential. All other details are irrelevant to me.

Virtus represents the next chapter for humanity. It is the era we are accelerating toward, where the exalted state of the Masculine archetype will become not just rare but prevalent—and, ultimately, a prerequisite for flourishing in a rebirthed soci-ety and advanced civilization that has risen into a higher octave of collective human consciousness.

However, no matter what humanity does collectively, the choice to rise into *Virtus* is yours alone. Only you can decide to take this path. Only you can do the work to transform yourself from *Homo Economicus* into an *Alpha Virtus*.

This is your task at hand, if you choose to become an Initiate.

The rest of this book is your field guide. In the chapters ahead, we'll explore the ten cornerstone qualities of the exalted Masculine archetype. For each virtue, we'll delve into its essence, its shadow state, and how it can be embodied in practical, real-world terms.

This is not a theoretical textbook to be memorized. It is a living guide—a framework for you to take into the real world and embody moment by moment. As you do, the old programming and faulty patterns within you will wither away, replaced by new neural pathways aligned with the virtues of *Virtus*.

Eventually, I hope this book becomes unnecessary to you—a stepping stone you outgrow and pass along to the next man who seeks the path. Because this work is about moving beyond the past and building the future.

Rome wasn't built in a day, but it was built. The same goes for you. It's time to start building—brick by brick, moment by moment.

This may be the most important work you ever do. For yourself first and foremost, but also as the highest contribution you could bestow upon your loved ones, your inner circle, and the entire mosaic of humanity—of which we are each a unique and invaluable puzzle piece.

Once you see, you cannot unsee.

THE CURRICULUM

"It's impossible for a man to learn
what he thinks he already knows."

—EPICTETUS

VIRTUE #1

ORDER

ALL TEN VIRTUES ARE EQUALLY VALUABLE, WOR-
thy, and important. Yet, Order is the only logical
place to start in this list of venerable qualities of the
Masculine archetype.

Order is at the very core of the Masculine, just as Chaos is at
the very core of the Feminine. Both are essential, complementary
forces within the Grand Architecture of Creation.

When we speak of Order in a spiritual context, we're not just
talking about the mundane tasks of organizing your life, such as
making your bed each morning—though that's a good habit, as
it brings your Masculine essence into the earthly realm. Spiritual

Order refers to something much deeper: stillness. This stillness, often called the "void," represents a perfect calm in your Inner World, regardless of the Chaos that inevitably arises in your Outer World.

The Outer World—the ever-changing, ever-evolving fabric of Creation—is inherently Feminine in nature and thus characterized by Chaos. As mentioned earlier, the Greek philosopher Heraclitus so wisely said, "Nothing is; everything is always becoming."

This means the Universe, our Outer World, is in a perpetual state of motion and transformation. Even things that appear static to us—mountains, for example—are constantly changing, albeit on a timescale beyond our perception. If we were to capture a 10-million-year time-lapse of a mountain, it would look more like a wave in the ocean than the seemingly solid structure we observe.

Any Order we try to find in the Outer World is, at best, an illusion. Life's inevitable disruptions—whether the loss of a loved one, a sudden financial crisis, or even the creeping effects of age—will eventually dissolve whatever Outer World Order we attempt to cling to.

Chaos is not the enemy—it's a known peril, a constant of life. And while we may not know the exact form Chaos will take, we can anticipate its arrival. Since we cannot change the Grand Architecture of Creation, the only true antidote to Chaos is to cultivate perfect Order in our Inner World.

Inner World Order—a perfect calm amid the storm—is a hallmark of the exalted Masculine. This is not a luxury or a "nice-to-have" feature. Order is the ultimate survival tool. When Chaos strikes, panic leads to poor decisions and jeopardizes not only your own well-being but also that of those in your care. Perfect calm, on the other hand, grants clarity of thought and allows you to navigate the storm masterfully.

To achieve this, you must become a true Stoic.

Modern society often misunderstands what it means to be a Stoic. It's not about shutting off your emotions or closing your heart. In fact, it's the opposite. The exalted Masculine feels every-thing—every emotion flows through him like a raging current—but he remains unshaken. His Inner World Order is immutable. This is what true Stoicism looks like.

Contrast this with the man who is triggered into Chaos when someone cuts him off in traffic. He flips the bird, shouts profan-ities, and stews over it for hours. This is a man with no Inner World Order. He is lost, as the affairs and circumstances in his Outer World own him.

Mastering Order is reclaiming a true Masculine superpower. Imagine *Being* so grounded in your Inner World that no exter-nal event can derail you. Picture a moment when your loved one, caught in a hormonal storm, unleashes her Chaos upon you. Instead of reacting defensively and escalating the situation, you remain calm, open-hearted, and fully present. Your clarity allows you to respond intuitively in a way that diffuses her storm. When Chaos meets Order, Order always prevails.

I could give you ten more crisis scenarios—whether as cata-strophic as a hurricane or as trivial as a spilled cup of tea—but it wouldn't change the principle. It doesn't matter what form Chaos takes; the exalted Masculine embodies Order wherever he goes. In every situation, in any environment, and no matter how Chaos manifests in his Outer World, he remains steadfast.

So, how does the true Stoic maintain Order? By commanding his Mind to pause.

The untrained Mind reacts compulsively to sensory inputs, defaulting to patterns buried deep within the subconscious. These reactions are often fear-based and suboptimal, driven by primal survival instincts. Our emotions—whether uplifting or negative—are merely visceral, bioelectrical expressions of our current thoughts. Emotions follow thoughts, even when we're not conscious of what we're thinking. These autonomous thought forms originate from the subconscious, which operates beyond our immediate awareness.

Sometimes, we notice the emotion first, but that doesn't mean thought didn't precede it—we just weren't aware of the thought form that triggered the feeling. This is why achieving calmness of Mind is critical: it's the lever that gives us access to regulating both our thoughts and the emotions they generate.

A master, however, knows how to press the pause button. He restores his Inner Order before thinking and then calmly responding with intention. This conscious response flows from the higher intelligence of the Heart, which whispers solutions that transcend the limitations of the rational Mind.

The Heart is the portal to the highest form of intelligence available to us—the intelligence that permeates the cosmos. Its language is not logic but feeling, sensing, intuiting, and direct knowing. When we remain open-hearted, this suprarational intelligence guides us with clarity and wisdom. We instinctively align with the optimal course of action, knowing what to say or do without hesitation.

But when Chaos invades our Inner World, these channels become blocked, and the neural circuitry of our Heart-Mind connection is short-circuited. When this occurs, it defaults us into operating from our primal Mind and its hard-wired basic survival instincts. Hijacked by emotions, we act impulsively, often making the situation worse or causing harm to ourselves and those around us as we react from the mental fog of our most base subconscious programming. Mastering Order keeps these channels open, ensuring that we remain a source of stability, wisdom, and strength—no matter the circumstances.

As a freshly minted Initiate, reclaiming Order is your first Masculine superpower.

Imagine a life where your Inner World is unshakable—where no external circumstance can derail your peace. Let's say some crisis or calamity—whether major or minor—meets you, as it inevitably will. Life is not only sunshine and roses. Perhaps it's a financial loss, your house burns down, or a dear friend dies in an accident. Maybe the woman you love unleashes her Chaos in a moment of emotional overwhelm.

No matter the form Chaos takes, instead of reacting defensively or escalating the situation, you remain calm, centered, and open-hearted. With perfect clarity, you intuitively sense how to lead the situation or interaction with wisdom, compassion, and strength. Whatever the storm, no matter how intense, it will inevitably dissipate in the presence of calm Order.

This is the power of embodying Order. When Chaos meets Order, Order always prevails.

No matter the crisis—whether it's catastrophic or merely a storm in a teacup—the exalted Masculine embodies Order wherever he goes. Chaos will arise; that's simply the nature of the Outer World. But when you've mastered Order, your presence becomes a beacon of stability in the midst of life's storms.

Once you see, you cannot unsee.

PRACTICE MAKES PERFECT,
MASTERY IS EARNED

VIRTUE #1: ORDER

The Three-Step Pause:
A Practical Exercise

1. Pause and Breathe
When faced with a moment of crisis or heightened emotion, immediately pause or stop whatever you're doing. Take a deep breath in through your nose for a count of four, hold it for a count of four, and then exhale slowly through your mouth for a count of six. Repeat this for three breaths. This simple act sends a signal to your nervous system to calm down.

2. Name the Chaos
Silently name what you're feeling or experiencing in one or two words. For example: "anger," "fear," "confusion," or "overwhelm." By naming the emotion or situation, you create a small distance between yourself and the reaction, giving your conscious Mind the space to regain control.

3. Ask: What's My Next Best Step?
Shift your focus to what needs to happen *next*—not the entire problem, just the next best step. This keeps you grounded and prevents spiraling into overwhelm. For

example, if you're in an argument, the next step might be staying silent and breathing. If it's a financial crisis, it might be making a phone call or reviewing your situation calmly.

LOVE

WHAT WOULD LOVE DO?
This is arguably one of the most meaningful—and therefore powerful—questions on Earth. It's the inquiry that cuts through the noise and brings us back to center.

When (not if) you master Order, this question becomes one of your primary tools any time life confronts you with challenges. It's a compass to navigate the storms of the Outer World, especially when your emotions threaten to hook you into your lower nature.

Your lower nature is the shadow side of your egoic Mind, which is sensitive, fragile, and easily triggered. Your Ego—also called the "small self"—always desires to be right. It thrives on righteousness and has a tendency toward derailing into victim-hood, descending into indignation at the smallest slight. When triggered, it spirals into anger, arguments, and crassness. If unchecked, it escalates into destructiveness, violence, or harm—justified by its self-centered narratives.

None of this adolescent chaos occurs when your Inner World is governed by Order. At the first hint of the Ego's descent into pettiness, Order steps in to restore balance.

Remember: Pause.

Order presses the pause button, arrests the Ego's fall into vic-timhood, restores calm, and allows you to respond intelligently from a place of equanimity. When a man has fully mastered Order, this process becomes instantaneous—a reflex ingrained deep in his subconscious. He embodies Order so completely that it becomes second nature.

From this place of perfect calm and Order, the question "*What would Love do?*" becomes extraordinarily powerful.[1] But before we explore why, we need to understand what Love truly is—and perhaps just as importantly, what it is not.

You'd think everyone knows the answer, but ironically, most people merely "think" they know. Few have engaged in a genu-ine inquiry into the nature of Love. For many, it's a word they've learned to spell and repeat, copying what others around them seem to believe about it.

---

1   Two other very powerful questions would be "What good in this situation am I failing to see?" and "What's my very best next step right here, right now [given the facts and circumstances I find myself in]?"

If that sounds familiar, take no offense. This is the starting point of growth. All great philosophers became who they were through inquiry. The word "philosopher" itself derives from "Philo," meaning Love, and "Sophia," meaning wisdom—literally, a "Lover of wisdom."

As an Initiate, you are invited to become a philosopher. This book is curated to help you fall in love with wisdom and embark on a never-ending journey of inquiry into all that matters most.

So, let's begin by making a simple philosophical inquiry into Love.

To avoid confusion, we must first recognize that not all Love is the same. There are two distinct essences of Love: one we'll call "Love (the emotion)" and the other "Love (the energy)." While we could just as easily label these as "conditional Love" and "unconditional Love," those terms carry preconceived meanings that might cloud our understanding. Instead, my aim here is to introduce you to Love as both a Power and an energy field—a force field with exquisite qualities and properties that we have the capacity to embody and express into the world.

For clarity, whenever I refer to "Love" in this book, I am exclusively speaking about Love (the energy). Whenever I use the word "love" I am referring to love broadly or in a generic sense. The only time I am specifically speaking about Love (the emotion) is here in this section.

These two types of Love are fundamentally different. In fact, they are more dissimilar than they are alike, as their essence originates from entirely different sources.

Let's pick apart Love (the emotion) first.

Love (the emotion) is what most people mistakenly believe to be Love. While there's nothing inherently wrong with Love (the emotion), it possesses two defining characteristics that distinguish it from the exalted Love (the energy):

- **Exclusion:** Love (the emotion) is inherently conditional and limited. We might "love" our race, culture, country, or favorite sports team—but not others. This doesn't necessarily mean we hate or harbor animosity toward those "others." More often than not, we're simply indifferent. However, this exclusivity makes it clear that Love (the emotion) is not the all-encompassing energy of Love (the energy), which, in its highest expression, knows no boundaries and excludes nothing.

- **Fleeting Nature:** Love (the emotion) is perishable and unstable. It ebbs and flows based on circumstances and conditions. For instance, we may "love" our spouse deeply at the altar, only for that same relationship to unravel into bitterness and animosity in a divorce court years later. This impermanence reveals Love (the emotion) to be more like a river—subject to overflowing, running dry, or shifting course—rather than the eternal, ever-present force of Love (the energy).

While Love (the emotion) is fleeting and conditional, it is not inherently bad. We are naturally wired to feel it, and it plays a vital, beautiful role in our human experience. It adds color, richness, and texture to our lives, and without it, our existence would feel flat and hollow. The problem arises only when we mistake or confuse Love (the emotion) with Love (the energy), failing to recognize the profound difference between the two.

Contrary to popular belief, the opposite of Love (the emotion) is not hate or fear—it's indifference. When Love (the emotion) leaves the building, what remains is indifference. We simply stop caring. Ironically, when we hate, we still care—a lot, albeit in a destructive and negative way. The true opposite of hate is not love of any kind but idolization or aggrandizement. Similarly, fear—a negative belief in the absence of concrete evidence—finds its opposite in faith, a positive belief in the absence of concrete evidence. Neither hate nor fear serves as the opposite of Love (the emotion). Trust me on this: the true opposite is indifference, and we can know this because of the unthinkable atrocities we continue to witness in the world.

Let's connect this to the unthinkable suffering I mentioned earlier. At its core, indifference is the principal cause. This collective indifference is why wars, violence, racism, inequality, injustice, famine, and poverty persist and often feel "normalized." As a society, we say we care—perhaps we donate a few dollars, post messages of concern on social media, or make passing comments of sympathy—but fundamentally, humanity remains plagued by a profound indifference to the suffering of others. This same indifference extends to the systemic ecocide of our planet. If we truly cared, we would stop kneeling at the Altar of Money and begin making more intelligent choices and embrace the changes we know must be made as individuals, as societies, and as a collective species.

This indifference is a direct result of our gross inability to access true Love (the energy). It's not that we lack compassion entirely—it's that collectively, mankind has not yet ascended to the level of spiritual ripeness and wisdom where we have the capacity to transcend our limited selves and extend Love (the energy) universally, beyond the narrow confines of our personal and immediate concerns.

Love (the energy) is of an entirely different essence than Love (the emotion). It is the exalted, all-encompassing force that animates and binds all of Creation. This is not a fleeting feeling or a conditional attachment; it is a power, an energy field, and a frequency. Love (the energy) is not subject to the laws of polarity—it has no opposite and exists beyond duality. It is absolute, eternal, and immutable.

Unlike Love (the emotion), which is exclusive and perishable, Love (the energy) is inclusive and ever-present. It knows no boundaries, no exclusions, and no limitations. It simply is. It does not falter or fade because it is not dependent on circumstances, conditions, or externalities. Love (the energy) is unconditional by its very nature.

To understand this, we must delve into a fundamental concept: polarity. In this universe, most things exist on a continuum with opposing poles. Hot and cold are opposite poles on the continuum of temperature. Somewhere in the middle, one transitions into the other, depending on perception and relativity. Similarly, Love (the emotion) and indifference are opposite poles on the continuum of emotional love.

But Love (the energy) is different. It does not belong to any continuum. It does not transition, waver, or shift. It simply exists in its absolute form. This is why it is the greatest power in the universe. It is, quite literally, Divine power—the creative and regenerative force behind all of existence.

When a man rises into the exalted Masculine archetype, Love (the energy) becomes accessible to him. It becomes the "sword" of his higher nature, a tool of profound transformation and healing. In embodying Love, he aligns himself with the Creator, Absolute, Most High, or whatever you wish to call it by becoming a living extension of the Divine. This is the very essence of being "created in His image."

With great power, however, comes great responsibility. To wield Love (the energy) is to take on the responsibility of service—not to become a martyr or a doormat, but to shift focus from self-serving pursuits to the betterment of the collective. To do so, a man must surrender all lower-nature tendencies: gluttony, debauchery, greed, personal gain, and all other forms of selfish indulgence. Only by becoming a pure vessel of Love (the energy) can he channel its limitless power.

Love (the energy) is not a romantic fairytale or a Disney-inspired fantasy. It is the highest order of intelligence and power in existence. As the great philosopher Heraclitus once said:

"What are men? Mortal Gods.
What are Gods? Immortal men."

Love (the energy) is not weak or sentimental—it is transformative, regenerative, and infinitely creative. Anything created, empowered, infused, bestowed, encircled, or embraced with Love inevitably heals, thrives, grows, flowers, blossoms, unites, harmonizes, regenerates, and manifests effervescent beauty in countless forms.

When a man embodies Love, he becomes a magnetic force of presence, depth, and charisma. People and opportunities naturally gravitate toward him—not because of what he has, but because of who he is *Being*. Love, as the highest frequency in existence and the very fabric of Consciousness itself, is what every human being craves, often without even realizing it.

No matter what he does in life or how big or small his personal circle of influence is, wherever he goes and whatever realm he enters, everything rises and is held to a higher standard. This is the power of Love (the energy): absolute, eternal, and incorruptible. For the exalted Masculine man, Love is not a theoretical concept or abstract ideal—it is the essence of his *Being* and the ultimate expression of his Soul.

None of this is easy—or convenient. It is neither simple nor expedient to witness the unthinkable and unfathomable suffering in this world and still find the capacity within your Heart to see beyond the personalities of those who offend or harm, to love the Divine essence within them that remains hidden from view.

It is not easy to refrain from judgment, to forgive, and to truly embody the credo Jesus uttered with his final breath: "Forgive them, Father, for they do not know what they have done."

The exalted Masculine man, risen above his own lower nature, has the capacity to see and understand what others cannot. He realizes that not all men have yet risen and that some remain lost in the shadows. They need his help—not his pity, judgment, or condemnation. They need his love and compassion above all else because, as we've concluded, Love is the only true medicine. It is the antidote to the pain, suffering, and ignorance that drives men in their lower nature to act like savages.

Does this mean becoming a "loving" doormat or tolerating oppression, abuse, or exploitation? Absolutely not. The exalted Masculine maintains firm boundaries and protects himself when necessary. But he does so with intelligence, not violence. He meets every situation with the clarity and integrity that comes from aligning with Love.

And so, we ask ourselves often: *What would Love do?*

Love will do what it has always done. It heals, thrives, grows, flowers, blossoms, unites, harmonizes, regenerates, and creates effervescent beauty in every form it touches.

That is the answer to every situation, as Love is our pathway to access universal intelligence and meet every situation or circumstance with wisdom, clarity, and compassion.

These are the Divine marching orders of the exalted Masculine archetype. This is what he does because it is who he has chosen to *Be*.

Once you see, you cannot unsee.

PRACTICE MAKES PERFECT,
MASTERY IS EARNED

VIRTUE #2: LOVE

Exercise: Embodying Love in Action

This simple, three-step exercise will help you cultivate the practice of embodying Love (the energy) in your daily life. It is designed to be actionable, practical, and immediately impactful.

Step 1: Pause and Ground Yourself in Order
Before you can access Love, you must first restore calm and Order within your Inner World. The next time you find yourself in a challenging situation, pause for a moment. Take three deep breaths, focusing entirely on the inhale and exhale. With each breath, imagine yourself becoming more grounded, steady, and still, as if anchoring yourself in the unshakable calm of your Masculine essence.

Step 2: Ask the Question
From this place of inner stillness, silently ask yourself: What would Love do? Take a moment to feel the situation, tuning into the energy of Love (not the emotion). This might mean approaching with compassion, offering understanding, or responding with kindness—even

if firm boundaries are required. Allow the answer to arise naturally, without forcing it.

Step 3: Take Loving Action
Once clarity comes, act from that place of Love. Whether it's choosing kind words, extending forgiveness, standing firm with grace, or simply holding space for another, ensure your actions align with the essence of Love: to heal, unite, and uplift.

Remember, acting from Love doesn't mean tolerating harm or neglecting your own well-being. Sometimes Love is expressed through firm but respectful boundaries or by walking away from a toxic situation. The key is to act with integrity, without judgment, and with the intention to serve the highest good.

Pro Tip: Begin practicing this exercise with smaller, everyday situations—a minor disagreement with a loved one, a frustrating delay, or a difficult conversation at work. Over time, you'll find this practice becomes second nature, allowing you to embody Love even in the face of significant challenges.

Love is the greatest power you can wield, and with practice, it will become your default state of *Being*.

VIRTUE #3

COMPASSION

I T MIGHT SURPRISE SOME THAT COMPASSION RANKS
so prominently in this curriculum of the exalted Masculine
archetype. Traditionally, we associate the ideal man with
superhero qualities like strength, bravery, courage, grit, and
perseverance. These are powerful and essential traits, but
Compassion stands apart because it requires something far
greater—our soulfulness.

Compassion is not reactive or automatic like strength or
courage, which are hardwired survival mechanisms triggered by
resistance or fear. Those traits kick in naturally when the amyg-
dala sounds the alarm, hypersensitive as it is to the smallest

infractions—like a mosquito buzzing in your ear. Compassion, by contrast, is deliberate and intentional. It requires us to transcend the primal reflexes of our lower nature and operate from the elevated consciousness of our soul.

Soulfulness is what separates humans from mere survival-driven creatures. It is our capacity to feel deeply, to empathize, and to recognize the Oneness of all things. And it is through the mastery of Compassion that we access and embody this soulfulness most fully. Without Compassion, a man may exhibit strength or grit, but he is still operating from his lower nature—reacting, defending, surviving. With Compassion, he steps into the realm of true Soul power, where his actions become guided by wisdom, love, and the higher purpose of service.

In a world that has groomed men to be soft, emasculated, and passive—through chemical attacks on testosterone levels and cultural narratives that blame all societal ills on men—Compassion is often misunderstood or dismissed as a weakness. Nothing could be further from universal Truth. Real Compassion is the opposite of weakness; it is the courageous act of transcending ego and choosing to lift others up, regardless of whether they "deserve" it or not.

Compassion is what enables the exalted Masculine man to see through the layers of conditioning, fear, and Chaos in others and to recognize their Divine essence and innate potential. It connects him to his Soul and strengthens his capacity to act as a force for good in the world. True Compassion is a deliberate choice. It is the hallmark of a man who has mastered his Inner

World and walks the path of soulfulness with clarity, grace, and unwavering strength.

At the same time, our society has spent decades grooming soft, weak, and emasculated men. The tools of this grooming are multifaceted: the tyranny of chemical-laced foods annihilating testosterone levels, the cultural narrative that endlessly blames men and their so-called "patriarchy" for all societal ills, and a world that increasingly values passivity over vitality.

Let's address the elephant in the room about "patriarchy." Yes, there's a ruling elite—let's say 1% of men for discussion purposes—who hold the lion's share of the real power, influence, and resources. But the other 99% of men are just as oppressed, indentured, and boxed in as anyone else. Even the "average Joe"—whether he's struggling to make ends meet or managing to scrape together a "comfortable" living—is chained to a system that keeps him domesticated, distracted, and disconnected from his true nature.

This system doesn't just oppress men; it conditions them to idolize their oppressors. Men are lured into passivity, taught to revere strength and courage from the sidelines through sports voyeurism, Hollywood superheroes, and celebrity worship while rarely embodying these virtues themselves. They've been sold the hollow ideal of the "good life," living to work and drowning in debt from houses, cars, and trinkets that serve only to numb their dissatisfaction.

For the better-paid working man, the trappings of this system are the same—just dressed up. The house is bigger, the cars are flashier, and the designer goods are more exclusive. But make no mistake: it's still a gilded cage. This is what we've been conditioned to call "living the dream." And the vast majority of us have bought into it wholesale.

Compassion, when applied to this situation, reveals a profound truth: these gunshot wounds may be self-inflicted, but they're inflicted within a rigged system designed to keep men blind to their chains. It's far easier to ridicule or condemn this blindness than to meet it with the strength of Compassion. Yet the exalted Masculine does not see these men as helpless victims doomed to flounder in the quicksand of their own lower nature. He sees their innate potential and asks, "How can I help lift them up?"

Each man holds the key to his own liberation. The only way out of this cultural quicksand—this system designed to keep men shackled to mediocrity—is through the cultivation of sovereign critical thinking. True sovereignty begins with the ability to examine the world beyond the confines of the belief systems we've inherited. It requires the courage to question everything: societal norms, cultural values, and even the identities we've constructed based on the expectations imposed on us.

This is no small task. We've all been shaped by the waters of the fishbowl we were born into. The values of our upbringing, the lessons of our education, and the narratives of our society seep into our subconscious by osmosis. Rarely do we stop to question whether these beliefs are true, let alone whether they serve our highest potential. Yet without this inquiry, we remain trapped—prisoners of a worldview we didn't consciously choose, swimming in a sea of invisible biases that dictate our every move.

Sovereign critical thinking is the antidote. It's the ability to step outside the conditioning, to observe it from a higher vantage point, and to dismantle the chains of inherited beliefs with Truth and clarity. This process requires immense honesty—not only with the world around us but also with ourselves. We must confront where we have conformed, where we have settled, and where we have allowed the system to dictate our values, priorities, and sense of self.

Compassion is the bridge that allows us to approach this process without condemnation. When we look at ourselves with Compassion, we see our conditioned self not as a failure but as a product of a system designed to keep us disconnected from our true power. This same Compassion then extends outward to others. When we recognize the quicksand we've been swimming in, we can see that others are trapped as well, often without even knowing it. And instead of judgment, we can meet them with understanding and encouragement.

This is how Compassion fuels liberation—not just for ourselves but for those within our circle of influence. When we embody true sovereign critical thinking, we become living proof that there is a way out. Our presence becomes an invitation for others to examine their own conditioning and reclaim their sovereignty. This is not just an act of personal liberation; it is an act of service to the collective.

I realize that sounds harsh, but it's actually the act of enabling, placating, or contributing to these poor decisions that lacks any Compassion. To understand this fully, it's helpful to delve a little deeper into the etymology of the word "Compassion."

Compassion comes from the Latin roots "com," meaning "with or together," and "compati," meaning "to suffer." At its essence, Compassion means "to suffer together," to feel another's pain as though it were your own. But what does that truly mean, especially in the context of soulfulness and sovereign critical thinking?

To feel another's suffering as your own requires a depth of self-awareness and empathy that transcends mere emotional reactions. It asks us to engage with the world not through the lens of our conditioned beliefs but through the lens of Truth. This is where sovereign critical thinking becomes essential. Without it, we are merely operating as products of the systems we were born into, reacting based on biases, prejudices, and inherited narratives. Sovereign critical thinking is the tool that allows us to strip away these layers, examine our own chains, and see others not as adversaries or "others" but as reflections of the same Divine essence that animates us.

When we apply this perspective to Compassion, it becomes clear that enabling poor decisions, placating harmful behaviors, or contributing to another's suffering is not Compassion at all. True Compassion is not passive; it is active and courageous. It calls us to take responsibility for how we show up in the world and how we engage with others, even when that engagement challenges the status quo or causes discomfort.

Compassion asks us to suffer *with* others—not in pity or condescension, but in the acknowledgment of shared humanity and the Divine spark within each of us. It requires us to look past our enculturated biases and societal programming to truly see and understand another person's pain and then respond to their pain with wisdom and integrity.

All change starts within. This is an immutable law of the universe. When we transform our Inner World, the Outer World inevitably mirrors and reflects these changes back to us. This is the alchemy of life: when we start making different decisions about who we are as men, we carve out new neural pathways that govern our habits, behaviors, and choices. And when we change our habits, everything—our relationships, circumstances, and opportunities—begins to shift.

Every man possesses this potential for transformation. Nothing about our lives is truly fixed or permanent; everything is subject to the decisions we make. But here's the catch: If you allow your lower nature to remain in the driver's seat, your choices will keep you trapped in a life of mediocrity and dependence. You'll be like a caged lion, powerful yet confined, reliant on the scraps thrown your way by the systems that domesticate and control you.

True freedom, power, and potential lie beyond the walls of this figurative cage, but they require the courage to rise above our lower instincts and societal conditioning. Without this courage, the safety and predictability of the cage may seem appealing—complete with the comforts of paid healthcare and the illusion of security—but they come at the cost of your soulfulness and sovereignty as a man.

Until we develop Compassion for our own inner wounds and confront the boyish, deflated parts of ourselves who are making poor decisions, we cannot begin to express the fullness of the exalted Masculine archetype. By owning our pain, healing our wounds, and making decisions from a place of clarity and strength, we reclaim our sovereignty and align with our higher potential.

Compassion must always start with the Self. Once you've confronted your own limitations, cured your impotence, and restored your sovereignty as a man, you can begin to express Compassion into the world from a position of *strength and vitality*. It's not just a choice—it's a duty. As a representation of the exalted Masculine, your presence in the world must uplift all others. Wherever you go, you must seek to make things better, more harmonious, more safe, more just, and more beautiful. It's really just that simple.

Now, note that this expression of Compassion comes from a position of *strength and vitality*, not *power and influence*. Not all men are destined to be titans of industry or political juggernauts, and that's perfectly fine. We each walk unique timelines, and all vocations are equally worthy when pursued to the level of mastery. Whether you're a firefighter, a nuclear physicist, a master plumber, or a CEO, the size of your circle of influence is irrelevant. What matters is how you show up within your unique sphere of impact—your family, community, workplace, or even just the people you encounter in passing.

Full and unconditional Compassion for Self is a major spiritual bridge to cross, but Compassion for all others in all situations is the vast, shark-infested ocean we must swim across. These "sharks" are the hard-wired entanglements of our Mind: the

reflexive tendencies toward separation, judgment, and classifi-
cation. Our Mind's default programming perceives everything in
terms of division—us versus them, right versus wrong—and ren-
ders judgment on every person, situation, or thing, no matter how
relevant or trivial. This is part of our survival instinct: an ancient,
primal mechanism that cannot be turned off but can be managed.

Managing this instinct requires sovereign critical thinking
and a profound connection to our soulfulness. Sovereign critical
thinking allows us to pause, examine our judgments, and question whether they arise from genuine discernment or from subconscious biases programmed by our upbringing, education, or
societal norms. Soulfulness, in turn, offers us the ability to connect to the Oneness of all Creation, to see beyond the superficial
divisions of our Egoic Mind, and to view the world through the
lens of Love and interconnectedness.

Our survival instinct—the part of us that sees everything as
a personal threat and reacts accordingly—must take a back seat
to the wisdom of the Heart. The Heart, unlike the Mind, does
not perceive separation. It has direct access to the Unity of all
things, allowing us to transcend fear and judgment. This is not
an easy task, but it is essential for the mastery of Compassion.
As we learned with the first Virtue, maintaining Order within
is a prerequisite for developing this higher perspective. Without
Order, the Mind runs unchecked, easily hijacked by its survival
programming.

Compassion demands that we rise above the Mind's default
reactions and reprogram ourselves to lead with the intelligence

of the Heart. This requires a willingness to confront our own conditioned beliefs and assumptions, as well as a deep commitment to embodying the truth that we are all interconnected. The exalted Masculine man understands this, and while he cannot erase the existence of the "sharks," he learns to navigate them with wisdom, discernment, and grace.

Compassion is the Swiss army knife of the exalted Masculine, a tool that allows him to rise above force, violence, and oppression. Remember, true Compassion is to feel another's suffering as if it were your own. When a man's entire frame and *Being* is saturated with Compassion, it becomes impossible for him to harm, oppress, exploit, or degrade others—whether for self-gain, out of ignorance, or in allegiance to some ideology, system, or false belief. He sees beyond the illusions of separation and understands that to harm another is, in essence, to harm himself.

This all-encompassing Compassion is not limited to individual humans. It extends to all groups—across races, creeds, religions, preferences, and nationalities—and equally to animals, Nature, and the entirety of Mother Earth. True Compassion does not pick and choose; it is not apportioned or compartmentalized. It is a state of *Being*, a conscious decision to embody and express Love as our essence in every interaction, every moment, and every situation.

To embody this universal Compassion is no small feat. It requires a man to transcend his lower nature and to step into his soulfulness—a higher octave of existence where he no longer acts from fear, selfishness, or greed. In this state, he no longer needs to cling to the false power of domination, control, or exploitation. Instead, his strength comes from his ability to uplift, harmonize, and heal. He becomes a guardian, a steward of the Earth and of the interconnected web of life that binds us all.

This is not just a lofty ideal; it is a practical and necessary expression of the exalted Masculine archetype. In a world rife with division, exploitation, and destruction, Compassion is the only force capable of mending the fractures and guiding humanity toward regeneration and harmony. It is not weakness but strength of the highest order. It takes courage to feel deeply, wisdom to discern what is needed, and sovereignty to act from Love (the energy) rather than fear.

So, what does all of this mean in daily life?

Compassion means we always seek the highest common good, the most intelligent solutions, and the greatest harmony in every situation. It means stepping back when necessary. It means leaving a situation instead of resorting to force or violence to achieve our way. It means understanding that "hurt people hurt people," so most often, turning the other cheek is not weakness but wisdom. Compassion is helping and uplifting others rather than finding ways to diminish or exploit them for personal gain. It is wielding forgiveness as our sword of choice, trusting that the universe will settle all karmic debts in ways far more intelligent and balanced than we ever could.

But make no mistake: Compassion is not submission. It does not mean becoming a doormat or tolerating oppression, abuse, or exploitation. As sovereign beings, we set firm boundaries and shield what is precious to us with integrity and fortitude. Compassion may compel us to leave relationships, jobs, or situations that no longer serve or honor us. It teaches us to protect ourselves and our inalienable rights without ever encroaching on the rights of others. The difference lies in how we act: using intelligence and wisdom rather than brute force or reactive violence.

For the Initiate, mastering Compassion is a strenuous test. It pushes every emotional button and challenges all the default programming of our lower nature. Yet, it is precisely because of this difficulty that Compassion is such a transformative game changer. When truly embodied, it supercharges our influence within our circle of life and transforms how we show up in the world.

The heartfelt Compassion of a man can change the arc of someone's life. It is a sacred medicine and one of the most vital forces our inverted and corrupted world desperately needs. Compassion, when fully embodied, becomes a profound act of soulfulness, a manifestation of sovereign critical thinking, and a demonstration of true Masculine strength. It is a calling, not an option, for those who seek to rise into their exalted nature.

Once you see, you cannot unsee.

> *PRACTICE MAKES PERFECT,*
> *MASTERY IS EARNED*

VIRTUE #3: COMPASSION

Exercise: Sovereign Critical Thinking as a Pathway to Compassion

To cultivate Compassion by using sovereign critical thinking to rise above reactive lower nature impulses, enabling thoughtful responses rooted in empathy, understanding, and wisdom.

Step 1: Pause and Observe Without Judgment
When you find yourself triggered—whether by someone's behavior, a situation, or your own thoughts—stop and pause. Use this moment to *observe* your initial reactions without acting on them. Ask yourself:
- What am I feeling right now?
- Why am I feeling this way?
- What assumptions or biases might be driving my reaction?

This creates a gap between stimulus and response, giving your Mind space to step out of its default programming.

Step 2: Question the Narrative
Engage your sovereign critical thinking by examining the broader context. Use the following questions as a guide:

- What might this person's or situation's perspective be?
- What beliefs, experiences, or struggles could be influencing their behavior?
- How might my own upbringing, societal conditioning, or personal biases be shaping my interpretation?

Challenge yourself to see beyond the immediate and surface-level story your Ego tells you. Seek the deeper truth or hidden pain behind the situation.

Step 3: Choose the Response of Compassion

From this expanded awareness, ask yourself the pivotal question:

- *What would Love (the energy) do?*

Let your response be guided by empathy, understanding, and a commitment to the highest good. Whether this means offering forgiveness, a kind word, constructive action, or simply walking away from a harmful situation with integrity, your choice will now come from a place of sovereignty rather than reactivity.

Reflection:

Regularly reflect on situations where you successfully applied sovereign critical thinking to act with Compassion. Notice how it affects your Inner World and your interactions with others. Over time, this practice rewires your default responses, allowing Compassion to become second nature.

INTEGRITY

IKE ALL VIRTUES, INTEGRITY IS NOT MERELY SOME-
thing we "have" but something we *become*. It saturates
our entire essence, radiating outward in every thought,
word, and action. When we embody Integrity, it's not just a char-
acteristic—it's our very *Being*, the foundation upon which we
build everything.

To say we "have" Integrity implies it's something we can gain,
cultivate, or acquire. In truth, we cannot merely possess it. We
must *become* it through a conscious decision—one that we then
solidify with unwavering commitment. This decision to embody
Integrity is the true test of mastery, as it demands consistency
regardless of circumstances, conditions, or consequences.

Mastering Integrity, then, is not about perfection but about the unwavering commitment to live by it. It requires a devotion to truth, to wholeness, and to the alignment of our thoughts, words, and actions. This high standard is what makes Integrity so rare in the world today, where convenience and compromise often take precedence.

Understanding why Integrity is such a cornerstone of the exalted Masculine archetype requires a deeper exploration of its origins. The word "Integrity" comes from the Latin "integritas," meaning soundness, wholeness, and completeness. Figuratively, it also refers to purity, correctness, and blamelessness. As the word evolved into Old French, it gained additional connotations of innocence and chastity.

At first glance, these qualities might seem pious or moralistic, but nothing could be further from the truth. Integrity's greatest utility is not found in religiosity or sanctimony but in its practical, enduring power. It serves as the bedrock of functionality in every domain of life. Without soundness and wholeness, nothing—whether it's a structure, system, relationship, or human being—can stand the test of time. A lack of Integrity inevitably leads to collapse, erosion, and failure.

Thus, Integrity is far more than a virtue; it is a necessity. It is the scaffolding that holds together all that we build and create, ensuring that what we construct will endure. And it is only through Integrity that we step fully into true manhood, leaving behind the fragmented boyhood that seeks shortcuts, excuses, and self-serving justifications.

Integrity is far more than a personal virtue; it is a universal principle that governs the very fabric of existence. When we examine Integrity in its truest form—soundness, wholeness, and alignment with truth—we realize that anything lacking it is doomed to falter. Be it a structure, system, or relationship, Integrity is the foundation upon which strength and longevity are built. Without it, the cracks may not appear immediately, but erosion is inevitable.

Now, consider the additional qualities tied to Integrity: innocence, purity, correctness, and blamelessness. At first glance, these may seem lofty or moralistic, but their essence is practical and powerful. Innocence points to a life free from undue harm caused to others. Purity speaks to the clarity of our intentions and actions. Correctness ties us to truth rather than falsehoods. And blamelessness is the natural state of someone living in alignment with their values. These aren't abstract ideals—they are the cornerstones of functionality and trust, both within ourselves and in our interactions with the world.

When a man lacks Integrity, everything around him begins to erode. Relationships break down. Trust dissolves. Systems fail. We see this on both personal and societal levels. In a world where Integrity is scarce, we are witnessing the devastating consequences: leaders who betray their people, corporations that exploit the environment and their customers, and institutions that crumble under the weight of their own corruption.

This decay may start small, but like a cancer, it has the propensity to spread. What begins as a single act of compromise or deceit can ripple outward, infecting everything it touches. A politician misuses public funds, and trust in government wanes. A corporation prioritizes profits over ethics, and entire industries become synonymous with greed. A man betrays a friend or a partner, and the bonds of trust unravel, leaving a wake of disconnection and loss.

Integrity, therefore, is not just a personal choice; it is a collective necessity. Every action we take and every decision we make—either contributes to the strength of the web of consciousness that connects us all or weakens it. And while we may not always have the power to change the Integrity of those around us—whether it's corrupt politicians, exploitative corporations, or broken systems—we always have the power to choose how we show up. This is our personal responsibility, and it is also our personal power.

When we embody Integrity, we send ripples into the cosmic ocean of consciousness, creating a mirrored reflection in our reality. Our actions matter. Our choices matter. And when we align ourselves with truth and wholeness, we become a beacon of strength, inspiring others to do the same.

Now, let's move on to "innocence, purity, correctness, and blamelessness" as the next layer of implied meaning within the word Integrity. At first glance, these qualities might seem tied to piety or religiosity, but that couldn't be further from the truth. What we're staring at is a core virtue whose greatest transcendent ripple effects lie in its unparalleled utility and functionality, not in sanctimonious ideals or priestly sainthood.

Innocence, in this context, points to causing no undue harm—being deliberate and conscious in thought, word, and deed. Purity speaks to the quality of our intentions, ensuring they are aligned with Truth and guided by the highest good. Correctness links directly to Truth itself, as opposed to Falsehoods, while blamelessness reflects a way of living where no fault can justly be ascribed to you. These are not abstract ideals meant for philosophers in ivory towers; they are practical, actionable qualities that form the bedrock of a life built on strength, authenticity, and wholeness.

These attributes—innocence, purity, correctness, and blamelessness—mark the transition from boyhood to manhood. They are the enduring qualities of a man who has stepped fully into his exalted Masculine archetype. In mastering Integrity, we don't just adopt an individual virtue; we step into the embodiment of manhood itself. This is the essential bridge that separates the self-serving ways of a fragmented individual from the unified strength of a man grounded in Truth.

And this is the whole point of Integrity: it is a direct path to maturity, wisdom, and the exalted Masculine archetype. The world today, with all its chaos, conflict, and corruption, reveals how rare this virtue has become. Integrity, once common among leaders and citizens alike, is now treated as an exception rather than the rule.

The mastery of Integrity leads us into true manhood and the embodied virtues of the exalted Masculine. Unwavering Integrity is a high bar, and the disarray we see in our world today makes it clear how rare and vital this virtue truly is.

A lack of Integrity lies at the root of wars, violence, crime, greed, and all forms of corruption. It erodes the very fabric of society, from institutions and corporations to relationships and personal ethics. When Integrity falters at the top—whether among politicians, corporate leaders, or cultural icons—it cascades downward, fostering mistrust and justifying self-serving behavior at all levels.

The lack or absence of Integrity is like a cancerous growth. What starts seemingly benign—such as small ethical compromises—quickly permeates and corrupts everything it touches. A politician engaged in self-dealing or a corporate leader prioritizing profits over humanity might seem removed from our personal lives, but these acts create ripple effects that poison the collective fabric of our society. When leaders fail in Integrity, it gives license to the rest of us to rationalize our own lapses, whether that's cheating on taxes, bending the rules for personal gain, or cutting corners in relationships.

Without Integrity, relationships—whether romantic, platonic, or professional—become unworkable. Trust erodes, and without trust, relationships cannot thrive. Conversely, when we collectively embody Integrity, society as a whole achieves unparalleled functionality and harmony. Integrity is not just the "right" thing to do; it is the intelligent thing to do, ensuring long-term sustainability and success.

Now, some might argue that issues like political corruption, corporate malfeasance, or societal decay are beyond their control. But this perspective fails to recognize the profound interconnectedness of all things. The reality we see in the Outer World is always a reflection of our Inner World, both individually and collectively. Each of us contributes to this shared reality with every thought, word, and action. If we were all in perfect Integrity, the world would transform accordingly. This truth underscores the personal power and responsibility each of us carries.

Integrity radiates a unique, energetic thumbprint that others intuitively sense. People might not consciously articulate why, but they instinctively trust, respect, and gravitate toward those who embody it. This is what makes Integrity a superpower. It turns a man into a natural leader, not through titles or declarations, but through the magnetic presence of his character. Integrity inspires trust and confidence on a subtle, energetic level, creating a ripple effect that elevates everyone within its sphere.

This magnetism extends into relationships, particularly with the Feminine. Women, in their natural wisdom, possess a profound ability to discern who they can trust and surrender their vulnerability to. A man of Integrity becomes a sanctuary of safety and trust. His very presence communicates reliability and strength, qualities the Feminine craves at the deepest level. This is why Integrity is a cornerstone of charisma and presence. It's not about external posturing or bravado but about an unshakable alignment with Truth that can be felt.

Integrity begins with the decision to embody it fully. While this decision can be challenging, we all have an innate compass that guides us. This intuitive sense warns us when we're about to stray from Integrity. It's not a question of learning something new but of reconnecting with what is already within us. When we commit to Integrity, this compass comes back online, guiding us toward choices aligned with our higher nature.

This decision to embody Integrity—day in and day out—is what transforms it from something we "do" into something we "are." It becomes the backbone of our essence, saturating every aspect of our life. This is why Integrity is a virtue we cannot afford to compromise on, no matter how tempting the shortcut, how alluring the self-serving decision, or how justified the rationalization might seem.

The rewards of living with Integrity are profound. Self-respect deepens, self-worth rises, and others instinctively recognize and respect the value we bring. Integrity creates a magnetic presence, elevating every relationship and endeavor. A man of Integrity becomes a lighthouse, illuminating the path for others.

And this luminous quality of Integrity isn't just a boon for personal fulfillment—it's the foundation of restoring balance and harmony in our relationships with the Feminine. For millennia, non-Integrous men have abused, violated, and oppressed the Feminine, creating deep wounds of mistrust. The only way to heal these wounds is through unwavering Integrity.

A man must lead with Integrity, proving through his consistent actions that he is trustworthy. Slowly but surely, this rewires the nervous system of the Feminine to trust again—not just him, but the Masculine as a whole.

When a man becomes truly Integrous, it's not something he needs to prove or declare. She will feel it. Integrity resonates as a frequency that penetrates the deepest layers of her *Being*, allowing her to surrender into the safety of his presence. This restoration of trust is sacred and essential for the coevolution of the Masculine and Feminine. It is a testament to the transformative power of Integrity when fully embodied.

Fortify your Integrity, and you'll find that everything else falls into place. It is the key to true leadership, the foundation of meaningful relationships, and the essence of a life well-lived. Become the lighthouse, the anchor, and the healer. Embody this treasured virtue, and watch how it illuminates and elevates everything and everyone you touch.

Once you see, you cannot unsee.

> PRACTICE MAKES PERFECT,
> MASTERY IS EARNED

VIRTUE #4: INTEGRITY

Exercise: Activating Your Integrity Compass

This exercise will guide you in recognizing, strengthening, and embodying Integrity in your daily life. Integrity is not just about avoiding wrongdoing; it's about aligning your actions with your highest values and becoming a source of trust, respect, and stability for yourself and others. By connecting with your innate Integrity compass, you'll develop the ability to navigate life with clarity and confidence.

Step 1: Reflect on Your Personal Alignment
Objective: Identify areas where your actions, words, and values align—and where they don't.
- Find a quiet space and take 5–10 minutes to reflect on the following questions:
    1. In what areas of my life do I feel fully aligned with my values?
    2. Where do I experience discomfort, guilt, or doubt about my actions or choices?
    3. Are there relationships or situations where I have compromised my Integrity?

- Write down your reflections without judgment. This is simply about gaining awareness of where you currently stand.

Step 2: Reconnect with Your Integrity Compass
Objective: Strengthen your intuitive sense of Integrity by tuning into your Inner World.

- Choose a recent situation where you felt conflicted about a decision or action.
- Close your eyes, take a deep breath, and recall the moment in detail. Focus on how it felt in your body. Did you feel a sense of ease and alignment, or was there discomfort or tension?
- This body awareness is your Integrity compass. Practice noticing this physical feedback in your everyday life to guide your decisions.
- Commit to pausing and checking in with your compass whenever you're faced with a choice that feels uncertain.

Step 3: Make a Daily Integrity Commitment
Objective: Take action to align your life more fully with Integrity.

- Every morning, choose one area where you can take a small but meaningful action to embody Integrity that day. For example:
  - Decline to participate in gossip at work.
  - Speak honestly but kindly in a challenging conversation.

- Avoid cutting corners on a task, even if no one is watching.
- Choose a product or service aligned with your values, even if it costs more or requires effort.
- At the end of the day, reflect on how it felt to embody Integrity in that instance. Notice any shifts in your sense of self-respect or confidence.

WISDOM

THERE'S A POETIC PARADOX WITHIN WISDOM: IT'S possible to know a great deal of information yet possess very little Wisdom. Conversely, one can hold profound Wisdom while knowing relatively little in terms of raw knowledge.

Of course, it's also possible to have neither or both. Those who lack both knowledge and Wisdom are often viewed as simple-minded, struggling with life as a constant uphill battle for mere survival. On the other hand, those who embody both become wise philosophers whose decisions and actions carry unparalleled effectiveness, fairness, and harmony with the rhythms of life.

To fully grasp the essence of Wisdom and uncover its deeper layers, we must explore three key concepts: **intelligence vs. unintelligence**, **content vs. context**, and **noble vs. ignoble**. Each offers a unique lens through which Wisdom can be understood, cultivated, and embodied.

So, let's start with "intelligence" vs. "unintelligence."

The implied meaning of intelligence and unintelligence may seem obvious, but humanity at large often misinterprets these terms. In our left-brain-oriented Western society, intelligence is closely associated with IQ—a measure of "smarts" or intellectual acuity. IQ measures our ability to solve puzzles, reason logically, and recall information. However, equating IQ with intelligence leads to a fundamental misunderstanding.

The reality is that individuals with high IQs—those often deemed the "smartest" among us—can (and quite often do) still make profoundly unintelligent choices. We see this clearly in the decisions of many political leaders, corporate titans, and other influential figures whose actions create destructive or degenerative outcomes. This disconnect between IQ and true intelligence highlights the need for a more universal definition.

In accordance with the immutable laws of the Universe, intelligence is defined as "that which produces intelligent outcomes." Intelligent outcomes are those that are conducive to the thriving of Life itself—life-affirming, regenerative, and net-positive for the greatest good of all. By contrast, unintelligence is defined as "that which produces unintelligent outcomes." These are actions or decisions that are life-denying, degenerative, or detrimental to the collective good.

Examples abound. War, violence, oppression, greed, fraud, pollution, and the ruthless exploitation of Earth's resources are all unintelligent outcomes. They do not affirm or sustain Life; instead, they degrade it. In light of this, we can no longer view intelligence as merely the capacity for rational thought or problem-solving. True intelligence is measured by the outcomes it produces and their alignment with the thriving of Life.

This universal definition of intelligence and unintelligence applies across all levels of existence. It governs how we steward the planet, navigate societal conflicts, lead organizations, and show up in our personal relationships. Wisdom, as we'll see, is deeply rooted in aligning our choices with intelligent outcomes, ensuring that our decisions are both life-affirming and harmonious.

Now that we've clarified the definitions of intelligence and unintelligence, we can examine real-world examples to illustrate their profound implications.

War, violence, oppression, hate, racism, greed, fraud, corruption, systemic inequalities, poor life habits, environmental degradation, and the reckless exploitation of Mother Earth are all unmistakable examples of unintelligent outcomes. None of these contribute to the thriving of Life itself. They diminish, degrade, and disrupt the delicate balance upon which all life depends. By definition, such outcomes stem from unintelligence, no matter how "smart" the architects behind them may seem.

This brings us to a sobering realization: Many of the political leaders, corporate titans, and scientists we consider the "smartest" among us—those who drive modern civilization—are not creating intelligent outcomes. Their actions often lead to disharmony, disruption, and degradation rather than regeneration and thriving.

The crux of the problem lies in our faulty definition of intelligence. When we equate intelligence with IQ or technical expertise while ignoring the life-affirming impact of outcomes, we make it possible for decisions to be rationalized yet profoundly unintelligent. Only by redefining intelligence in alignment with the Universal principle of harmony—where choices serve the greatest good of all—can we hope to arrive at truly wise and intelligent decisions.

This shift in definition has far-reaching implications, impacting how we steward the Earth, navigate geopolitical conflicts, structure our economies, and even interact in our personal relationships. Intelligence must be reoriented toward harmony, regeneration, and the thriving of Life at every level of existence.

By understanding this, we take the first step toward aligning our actions with Wisdom. We must examine not just the content of our choices but also their context, ensuring that our decisions are guided by principles that foster balance and harmony, both within ourselves and in the world around us.

Let's now take a closer look at "content" vs. "context."

All information, knowledge, and know-how—including every discipline of science and every technological breakthrough—falls under the realm of content. Content is what we study, learn, accumulate, and master. It serves as the engine for the advancement and evolution of human civilization, and there's nothing inherently wrong or harmful about content itself.

However, content is not enough. When divorced from context, it can become dangerous, misused, or even destructive. Context is the lens through which we discern the best application of content. It is the framework that informs how, when, and why we apply what we know.

For example, nuclear technology is content. Whether we use it to build power plants that generate clean energy or to create weapons of mass destruction depends entirely on context. Fracking technology offers access to oil and gas but at the cost of environmental degradation. Surveillance systems enhance security but can erode privacy and personal freedoms when misused. Without the guiding hand of context, content can too easily serve short-term gains at the expense of long-term harmony.

Context provides the wisdom to navigate these choices. It allows us to evaluate not only the immediate benefits of a decision but also its ripple effects on the web of life. Without context, content is a ship without a rudder, easily steered toward expediency, convenience, or personal gain rather than the greater good.

This imbalance is particularly evident in our Western capitalist societies, where decisions are often driven by near-term profits or personal advancement. On a micro-level, many of us prioritize our individual comfort over the collective well-being. We vote for policies that serve our immediate interests, ignore the ecological impact of our consumption, and bypass opportunities to contribute to something larger than ourselves. These are choices made in the absence of context, choices that ultimately lead to disharmony.

When content is placed within proper context, however, it aligns with the principles of Wisdom. It fosters solutions that not only address immediate needs but also preserve and enhance the harmony of the whole. This alignment is what allows us to balance innovation with responsibility, ambition with compassion, and progress with preservation.

In this way, context becomes the bridge between content and harmony, ensuring that our knowledge serves Life itself rather than undermining it. Only through this interplay of content and context can we consistently make decisions that reflect true intelligence and Wisdom.

What the above reveals is the very reason why Wisdom cannot be taught, learned, or memorized. Wisdom, like everything in this Universe, is dynamic, fluid, and ever-evolving. Nothing in Life is static, and both content—the information available to us—and context—the circumstances surrounding that information—are constantly shifting. This is why Wisdom transcends mere knowledge; it requires acute insight and attunement to the present moment. Wisdom dances with the harmonies and rhythms of Life, aligning itself with what is intelligent, regenerative, and life-affirming. It is perpetually focused on seeking the greatest good for all concerned, never confined to rigid formulas or preconceived notions.

Wisdom also carries hallmark signatures that serve as valuable clues. It is often rooted in simplicity, elegance, and grace—qualities that reflect the underlying order of Truth. Wisdom resonates deeply in our gut because it aligns with Truth, not the illusions or Falsehoods conjured by our Egoic Mind. Even when Wisdom delivers a hard or uncomfortable Truth, it is often respected and accepted because Truth is undeniable and self-evident to the Soul.

Moreover, Wisdom is saturated in goodness, as it originates from Love. This connection to Love explains why the profound question, "What would Love do?" often leads us directly to wise and intelligent decisions. Wisdom, in its purest form, seeks harmony, unity, and the flourishing of Life itself.

The texture of Wisdom: "noble" vs. "ignoble"

Wisdom has a texture, a distinct tapestry that carries with it a sense of the noble—a dignified, refined quality that reflects alignment with the laws and principles of the Universe. True Wisdom feels clean, pure, and unquestionable in its authenticity. It resonates deeply within us, not as a product of cultural conditioning or religious dogma, but as something eternal and universal.

While morals and ethics serve as guideposts for behavior, they are often colored and heavily biased by the cultural, societal, and religious frameworks we inherit. Morality in one society may differ vastly from that in another, and what is deemed ethical in one era may be condemned in the next. This is why Wisdom cannot rely solely on externally imposed rules or codes of conduct. Instead, it aligns itself with something far greater: Natural Law.

Natural Law operates beyond human constructs, reflecting the fundamental principles of this Universe. Its essence is captured in the Universal ethos of humanity, which is perhaps best expressed by the Golden Rule: "Do unto others as you would have them do unto you." The Golden Rule's presence across all major religions and ancient wisdom traditions is no coincidence. It reflects a truth so universal and timeless that it transcends cultural and historical boundaries. When we act in accordance with this ethos, we are stepping into the noble, the exalted, and the dignified.

But how do we discern what is noble versus ignoble?

The answer lies in our capacity for intuitive knowing. Noble actions—those that align with the higher intelligence of the Heart—are something we can feel, sense, and intuit. Even when faced with morally or ethically ambiguous situations, we often sense when we are acting from a place of Nobility versus when we are succumbing to the lower, self-serving impulses of our Egoic Mind. Ignoble actions, on the other hand, carry a distinct heaviness, a sense of dissonance that lingers within us, even when we attempt to rationalize them away.

It's important to understand that Nobility in action does not necessarily equate to comfort, ease, or the absence of harm. For example, choosing to euthanize a deeply loved but mortally sick pet is an excruciating decision. It involves taking a life, which is undeniably a form of harm. Yet, within the depth of our Hearts, we intuitively know this is the noble course of action—guided not by logic alone but by compassion and the desire to alleviate suffering. The ignoble choice would be to avoid the discomfort of the decision, allowing the animal to endure unnecessary pain.

This sense of Nobility goes beyond intellect. It is rooted in the suprarational intelligence of the Heart, which speaks to us through feelings, sensations, intuition, and direct knowing. While the rational Mind is bound by linear thinking, the Heart perceives reality in a multidimensional way, tapping into the harmonies and rhythms of the cosmos. It whispers truths that cannot always be deduced logically but are nonetheless undeniably correct.

Nobility is a compass, and we all possess it, even if we sometimes stray from its guidance. It is that innate sense of dignity and goodness that calls us to rise above our lower nature, to transcend personal gain, and to act in service of the greater whole. When we pause and listen to the intelligence of our Heart, we often find that the noble path is not only the wisest but also the most aligned with the harmony of the Universe.

Wisdom, therefore, is not a matter of adhering to societal norms or rigid ethical codes but of aligning ourselves with the Nobility that resonates within. It is about cultivating the discernment to recognize the difference between the noble and the ignoble in every situation and having the courage to act in accordance with that recognition—even when it's difficult, uncomfortable, or counterintuitive to our immediate desires.

Just as the texture of Wisdom is inherently noble, the exalted Masculine archetype radiates an aura of Nobility—not as a reflection of aristocracy, wealth, or societal status, but as the unmistakable presence of impeccable character. This Nobility transcends material markers such as money, titles, or rank, resting instead in the integrity, depth, and authenticity of the man himself.

To conclude, we would be remiss to ignore the relationship of life experience to Wisdom. While younger people undoubtedly possess the capacity to make wise decisions, Wisdom itself is something that ripens within us over time, much like a fine wine. We are each a mosaic of our life experiences, and the more experiences we have lived through—both the triumphs and tribulations—the more "content" and "context" we have to draw upon. There is no substitute for having walked many paths, faced diverse challenges, and accumulated the scars and insights that only time and lived experience can provide.

This is why many Indigenous cultures revered age and saw Elders as the stewards of Wisdom. Their life experiences were treasures to be shared, preserved, and passed down through the oral tradition of storytelling, which over time became the entire treasure trove of mythology about mankind. These stories, rich with nuance and meaning, were how they conveyed the essence of Wisdom across generations. In these societies, age was a marker of ripeness and readiness to guide others, a reminder that Wisdom is distilled through the alchemy of time, reflection, and growth.

Contrast this with our modern era, where information is ubiquitous, and anyone with an internet connection has access to more data than kings and presidents had just decades ago. Yet, the trap of this digital age is mistaking the volume of information for Wisdom. True Wisdom doesn't lie in the sheer accumulation of facts but in the ability to discern, synthesize, and align decisions with the greater good.

This should never discourage the young from seeking or practicing Wisdom. You are never too young to make wise choices, but Wisdom in unfamiliar territory often comes in recognizing the need to seek guidance. It lies in having the humility to consult those who have walked the path before us, listening not just to their words but to the layers of meaning and insight woven into their experiences. In this way, we reclaim the profound practice of honoring the Elders, not as relics of the past but as living bridges to timeless truths that enrich our own journeys.

Wisdom is also understanding that no matter where we are on the journey of Life, we are always both a student to some and a teacher to others, which often corresponds to age and Life experience but doesn't have to. Even these roles are not static or fixed, and Wisdom is having the intelligence to know when we're the student and when we're the teacher.

Once you see, you cannot unsee.

PRACTICE MAKES PERFECT,
MASTERY IS EARNED

VIRTUE #5

Exercise: Practicing Noble Decision-Making

This exercise is designed to help you consciously align your decisions with Wisdom by proactively choosing noble actions in your daily life. Through this practice, you'll strengthen your ability to act with dignity, respect, and alignment with the greater good.

Step 1: Identify an Upcoming Decision
- Think about a situation or decision you will face in the next 24-48 hours. This could be a conversation you anticipate, a choice you need to make at work, or even how you plan to spend your time.
- Write down what the decision entails and the possible options you're considering.

Step 2: Discern the Noble Path
- Pause for a moment and connect with the intelligence of your Heart. Bypass the surface-level chatter of your Ego and ask yourself:
  - Which choice aligns with dignity, integrity, and the greater good for all involved?

- Which choice reflects Love, harmony, and respect—even if it requires personal discomfort or sacrifice?
- Which choice feels noble in your gut and resonates as Truth?
- Be honest with yourself about which options might lean toward convenience, avoidance, or self-serving motives, and let that awareness guide you.

Step 3: Commit to the Noble Action

- Decide on the noble path forward and write it down as a clear commitment. Include why it's the best choice, not just for you but for the situation as a whole.
- Before taking action, visualize the ripple effect of this noble decision. Imagine how it will contribute to harmony, build trust, and reflect the Wisdom of your highest self.

By consciously choosing the noble path in real time, you strengthen your connection to Wisdom and align your actions with the greater good. Over time, this practice becomes second nature, empowering you to embody the exalted Masculine in every decision.

TEMPERANCE

WITHIN TEMPERANCE LIES A QUESTION AS OLD as humanity itself: Who owns who? Do our cravings and desires own us, or are we their master?

Temperance is often misunderstood as deprivation or self-denial. In truth, it is about mastery, harmony, and alignment. It is the conscious decision to engage with the material, mental, and emotional realms in a way that serves our highest potential rather than enslaving us to our lower nature.

Here, it's important to distinguish between harmony and balance. Balance implies a fixed or static point in time and space, whereas Life itself is ever-changing, ever-evolving, and always becoming. Balance, then, is not an immutable principle within the laws of Nature; harmony is. Harmony is dynamic and fluid, ebbing and flowing with the rhythms of Life itself. We see this reflected in every aspect of Nature, from the seasons to the ever-shifting dynamics of our relationships.

Temperance, too, must be understood as a practice of harmony, not rigidity or dogmatism. There are times in Life to fast and times to consciously feast and indulge. The harmony within Temperance lies in the intelligence and wisdom to recognize when we have moved into disharmony and self-correct. Disharmony often manifests as sickness, stress, overwhelm, or depression—a signal that we have deviated from the natural flow of Life.

This mastery of Temperance yields vitality—a vibrant and dynamic state of being that is the natural byproduct of living in alignment with harmony. By practicing moderation, we not only strengthen our physical body but also sharpen our mind and cultivate emotional resilience. Temperance, then, becomes a pathway to unlocking our magnanimous nature—the great Soul within each of us.

Before we delve into Temperance in earnest, let's first create the proper context. There's no need to judge the way success is measured in the material realm—trophies, fame, fortune, and applause are not inherently wrong. However, it's crucial to understand that the "game Man plays" is a Finite Game that always exists within the broader "game Spirit plays," which is the eternal Infinite Game.

Challenges arise when we fail to see the interplay of these two games or when we get lost in either one. The first challenge—unawareness of the Infinite Game—occurs when we are still unawakened from the dream of Life. For most, the "truth serum" of awakening hasn't yet dropped, and this happens only through the invisible hand of a Higher Order, in perfect timing for each person's journey. There's no hierarchy here—awakening does not make anyone better or more worthy, only different in their level of awareness. For those still unawakened, the Infinite Game remains unknown, and the only reality is the Finite Game.

Within the Finite Game, some retain their natural innocence, playing with honesty and integrity, while others fall prey to the shadow aspects of greed, fraud, and dishonesty. These behaviors aren't a reflection of "being lost" but are part of their unique lesson plan for this lifetime. Each person has their own plan, and our role is not to judge but to remain focused on our own path.

The second challenge occurs post-awakening. Once we see the Infinite Game, it's possible to lose ourselves in either one—whether by over-identifying with the material world or by bypassing it altogether in favor of spiritual detachment. Both states represent a disconnection from the purpose of life, which is to integrate, harmonize, and master these two realms, playing them simultaneously in alignment.

To be lost in the Finite Game is to forget our spiritual essence, while to be lost in the Infinite Game is to bypass our carnal, human nature—a phenomenon known as "spiritual bypassing." The purpose of Temperance is to bring harmony between these two games, enabling us to fully engage with life as both spiritual and physical beings.

With this foundational understanding, let's delve deeper into Temperance by first examining the poison of gluttony.

Gluttony, at its core, is the relentless pursuit of excess. It is the ravenous craving for more—more food, more pleasure, more material possessions, more stimulation—beyond what we genuinely need to thrive. The dictionary defines gluttony as an insatiable hunger, lust, or greed. It's not merely about satisfying a healthy appetite; it's about crossing the line into overindulgence and excess.

This is where the true poison of gluttony lies: As our cravings grow, they begin to own us. We fall into a pattern of overconsumption, not only physically but also mentally and emotionally, and we unknowingly give away our sovereignty to our desires.

In the physical realm, we see gluttony manifest in the form of obesity, lethargy, addiction, and a general lack of vitality. Overeating, excessive drinking, drug use, and the relentless pursuit of material possessions create a life weighed down by the burdens of indulgence. When we consume beyond our body's needs, we rob ourselves of energy and vibrancy, replacing them with sluggishness and decay.

But gluttony doesn't stop at the physical. It seeps into our mental and emotional realms, often unnoticed. Mentally, gluttony shows up as overstimulation—scrolling endlessly through social media, binge-watching television, or compulsively consuming information without purpose or discernment. The mind becomes dull, cluttered, and overwhelmed, unable to focus or find clarity. Emotionally, gluttony arises when we seek constant validation, drama, or emotional highs, leaving us numb, drained, and disconnected from our true selves.

The disharmony caused by gluttony is not just personal; it ripples outward. We live in a society built on this poison, where consumerism and instant gratification are celebrated. Debt-driven consumption of frivolous goods and luxuries—often purchased with money we don't have—becomes normalized. This keeps us enslaved to a system designed to feed off our gluttonous cravings, perpetuating the illusion that happiness lies in acquiring more.

The antidote to this poison is Temperance. It's the realization that fulfillment does not come from acquiring more but from desiring less. As the Stoic philosopher Epictetus so aptly put it: "Wealth consists not in having great possessions, but in having few wants." When we free ourselves from the chains of excess, we reclaim our vitality, clarity, and peace.

It's important to emphasize that Temperance does not mean rejecting the pleasures of Life or denying ourselves joy. It is about knowing when enough is enough. It is the wisdom to discern what nourishes us from what enslaves us and the intelligence to restore harmony when we stray into disharmony. There's a time to feast and a time to fast. Temperance allows us to engage with both in alignment with the rhythms of Life.

Ultimately, Temperance is not just a virtue; it is a pathway to sovereignty. When we are no longer ruled by our cravings and desires, we unlock a vitality, mental clarity, and emotional resilience that elevates us to our highest potential.

The path to Temperance is not about rigid restraint or living in deprivation—it is about harmony, intelligence, and sovereignty. When we fall prey to gluttony, whether physical, mental, or emotional, we lose our autonomy. We become enslaved to cravings, impulses, and desires, allowing them to dictate the course of our lives.

In truth, the virtue of Temperance is not about renouncing the pleasures of life but engaging with them consciously. It invites us to participate fully in the material realm without being consumed or owned by it. It's the difference between enjoying a feast with friends to celebrate life and falling into habitual overeating as a coping mechanism. Temperance is not a denial of joy—it is a pathway to vitality.

This is where the deeper essence of Temperance emerges: it cultivates vitality. Vitality is not merely physical health or energy; it is a holistic state of vibrancy that emanates from alignment in mind, body, and spirit. Gluttony of the mind—overindulging in constant information, distractions, and superficial entertainment—leaves us with a dull, foggy mind. Gluttony of the emotions—chasing drama, addiction to emotional highs and lows, or excessive attachment—leaves us emotionally drained and disconnected. In contrast, Temperance sharpens the mind and steadies the emotions, creating space for true clarity, creativity, and connection.

Temperance, then, is not about denial but balance in action—knowing when to feast and when to fast. It's the art of knowing when indulgence serves the Soul and when it burdens it. This dynamic harmony allows us to live life fully without losing ourselves to the excesses of the Outer World.

To master Temperance is to master the interplay between the many Finite Games and the one Infinite Game of life. These Finite Games are deeply rooted in the material realm: we pursue goals, acquire resources, and experience worldly pleasures. Every aspect of Life that we engage with in our Outer World—whether love, relationships, family life, friendships, careers, or personal aspirations—is part of these Finite Games. Many, if not most, of these aspects of Life are profoundly beautiful, enriching, and catalytic for growth and transformation, whether through inspiration or suffering. Hence, these pursuits are not inherently wrong. In fact, we are meant to fully engage with Life, as it is this engagement that brings us alive. However, when these pursuits consume us or, worse, begin to own us— when we cannot detach from them—they inevitably become a source of suffering.

The Infinite Game, by contrast, is the broader spiritual journey that transcends the physical world. It is the eternal dance of our Soul, where growth, expansion, and harmony with our Source are the ultimate pursuits. This one Infinite Game represents the Grand Odyssey of our Soul, spanning eternity and countless lifetimes. The Finite Games we engage with are the individual adventures and experiences that make up the arc of this eternal journey through time and space. Temperance is the virtue that bridges and harmonizes these two realms. It allows us to savor the fruits of the Finite Games without losing sight of the Infinite Game. It enables us to embrace and participate in the material world while staying deeply rooted in our higher self.

Mastering Temperance does not mean abandoning ambition or pleasure; rather, it means approaching them with wisdom, intention, and discernment. Temperance empowers us to choose wisely, to act from a place of alignment, and to create a life that reflects our highest potential. Through Temperance, we reclaim our sovereignty, becoming the master of our cravings and desires rather than their servant.

In essence, the wealth of Temperance is a richness of spirit that far outweighs the fleeting pleasures of indulgence. It is a state of sovereignty, where we are no longer owned by our desires but instead wield them as tools for creation and joy. Temperance does more than balance indulgence and restraint—it creates a pathway to rediscover the innate richness of our human experience. Through Temperance, we begin to see that true abundance does not come from accumulating or consuming endlessly but from gaining the eyes to perceive the beauty and wonder that exists in every moment of life.

Temperance opens the door to a deeper awareness of the extraordinary in the ordinary. A simple blade of grass, glistening with morning dew, can captivate us and kindle a sense of wonder far richer than any material excess could ever provide. It is through this lens that we realize the abundance and richness of life are already woven into its very fabric—always present, always available, and simply waiting for us to notice.

This is the deeper power of Temperance. It is not merely a practice of moderation but an art of living that grants us access to the fullness of existence. It creates the canvas upon which we can paint a life infused with vitality, wonder, and harmony, free from the burdens of craving and excess. In Temperance, we don't just simplify our lives; we amplify our capacity to experience the profound richness that is already here.

Once you see, you cannot unsee.

PRACTICE MAKES PERFECT,
MASTERY IS EARNED

VIRTUE #6: TEMPERANCE

Exercise: Conscious Choices—
Aligning Desire with Highest Good

The objective is to bring awareness to your choices, understand the motivations behind them, and consciously align your actions with what serves your highest good.

Step 1: Pause and Ask

Before you act on a desire—whether it's reaching for a snack, buying something, or reacting emotionally—pause and ask yourself two simple questions:

1. **Do I want this, or do I need this?**
2. **Why do I want or need this?**

Write down your answers or reflect deeply. Explore whether your action stems from:

- Escaping or numbing (e.g., stress, boredom, or anxiety).
- A craving that is driven by habit or impulse.
- A conscious desire that aligns with your highest good in this moment.

Step 2: Evaluate the Impact

Once you've identified the motivation behind your desire, assess the impact of your choice. Ask yourself:

- **Does this choice honor my vitality and well-being?**
- **Will this action bring me closer to harmony or push me further into disharmony?**
- **Am I choosing this with awareness, or am I on autopilot?**

This step is about becoming attuned to the ripple effects of your choices, not only on your body and emotions but also on your mental clarity and overall sense of alignment.

Step 3: Consciously Choose and Own It

Make your decision with full awareness and own it without guilt or shame. Whether you indulge, abstain, or find a middle ground, let your choice be deliberate. If you decide to indulge—say, enjoy that big meal and finish the bottle of wine—fully revel in the experience. Savor it without judgment.

Alternatively, if you recognize the choice is an escape or doesn't serve your highest good, honor yourself by choosing differently and feel empowered by your restraint.

Optional Reflection:

At the end of the day, take a few minutes to journal about your conscious choices. Reflect on how they impacted your vitality, harmony, and sense of fulfillment. Over time, this practice will naturally guide you to more aligned decisions.

NOBILITY

NOBILITY, IN ITS TRUEST SENSE, IS NOT A MATTER of birthright, aristocracy, or social status. It is not defined by titles, wealth, or the privileges society often associates with the noble class. Instead, Nobility is an intrinsic quality—a state of being that exudes elevated character, self-respect, and dignified conduct. It is an unshakable inner majesty that transcends the superficial markers of external success.

The signature of true Nobility is subtle yet unmistakable. It carries an aura of majesty and impeccability, a quiet yet profound presence that others intuitively recognize. It is the kind of energy that makes people feel seen, respected, and valued in your presence without the need for a single word. This essence is not taught, claimed, or bestowed—it is cultivated through the mastery of one's character and a deep alignment with the virtues that define the exalted Masculine archetype.

Nobility stands apart from the superficial trappings of societal status because it does not rely on outward validation. It is anchored in authenticity, self-respect, and an unwavering commitment to what is right, true, and just. A noble man is not swayed by applause or approval, nor is he diminished by criticism or rejection. His sense of worth is rooted in his alignment with higher principles, not fleeting external accolades.

At its core, Nobility reflects a man's capacity to embody his highest self in every situation. It is a quality that manifests in how he carries himself, the words he chooses, and the actions he takes. This is what makes Nobility an integral part of the exalted Masculine archetype. It is not about dominance or control but about presence, grace, and the unshakable strength that comes from a well-ordered Inner World.

This elevated state of being has a ripple effect. Those who encounter a noble man are often left with a sense of admiration and respect. His presence alone inspires others to rise to a higher standard, to act with greater integrity, and to bring more dignity into their own lives. In this way, Nobility becomes a quiet yet powerful force for transformation—not through loud proclamations but through the silent example of a man who is aligned with his highest virtues.

Nobility, then, is more than just a virtue. It is the crown jewel of the exalted Masculine—a state of being that carries an unspoken promise to elevate all that it touches.

True Nobility is built upon a foundation of virtues: humility, honor, generosity, grace, majesty, and genuine heartfelt concern for the world around him. These qualities are the bedrock of a noble man's character, forming the pillars that uphold his presence in the world. Without these virtues, Nobility is a hollow shell, a performance rather than a true expression of elevated character.

Humility is perhaps the most misunderstood of these virtues, often mistaken for meekness or weakness. In truth, humility is the quiet confidence that comes from knowing one's strengths without the need for boastfulness. It is the ability to stand tall without diminishing others, to recognize one's accomplishments without seeking validation, and to acknowledge one's imperfections without shame. A noble man is humble not because he thinks less of himself but because he is free from the compulsion to prove his worth to anyone.

Honor is the guiding compass of a noble man's actions. It is the commitment to do what is right, even when it is difficult or inconvenient. Honor demands consistency between one's words and actions, creating a trustworthiness that others can rely upon. A man of honor does not waver in his integrity, for he understands that his word is his bond and that his reputation is built not on fleeting achievements but on a lifetime of principled living.

Generosity, in the context of Nobility, extends far beyond material giving. It is the willingness to share one's time, energy, and presence with others. It is the open-heartedness to offer kindness, encouragement, and wisdom without expectation of reciprocity. A noble man's generosity uplifts those around him, creating a ripple effect of goodwill and abundance.

Grace is the virtue that softens strength, turning it into a magnetic force that draws others closer. A man with grace moves through life with poise and composure, unshaken by life's storms. Grace is not about perfection but about the ability to navigate challenges with elegance and dignity. It is the quiet assurance that, no matter the circumstance, one can rise above petty conflicts and meet adversity with wisdom and compassion.

The unmistakable aura or texture of Nobility is a sense of majesty, the ineffable quality that sets a noble man apart from a base man. Majesty is not about superiority or entitlement; it is about the radiant presence that emanates from a man who has mastered himself. It is the intangible yet palpable energy of someone who embodies self-respect, self-mastery, and alignment with higher principles. Majesty cannot be faked or forced; it is earned through the lifelong cultivation of virtues and the relentless pursuit of one's highest potential.

Finally, at the very core of Nobility lies a genuine, heartfelt care and concern for the world around him. His heart remains open, allowing him to feel deeply into the currents of life, including the suffering and struggles of others. This capacity for empathy is not a source of weakness but a profound strength, as it is balanced by his mastery of the exalted Masculine archetype. He feels everything—the joy, the pain, the hope, and the despair of the world—but none of it disturbs his Inner Order. He becomes a steadfast presence, like a rock in a wild river, unshaken yet fully immersed. From this place, he expresses his compassion not through pity or despair but through purposeful action, offering support and upliftment wherever he can. His care for others inspires trust, respect, and admiration, creating an unspoken but unmistakable bond with those he encounters.

Nobility, therefore, is not a singular virtue but the harmonious integration of these foundational qualities. Together, they create a man who is not only respected but deeply trusted and admired. This is why Nobility is so closely tied to leadership. A noble man does not lead through coercion or authority but through example. His actions speak louder than his words, and his character inspires others to follow willingly.

This type of leadership is rare in today's world, where the loudest voices often drown out the wisest ones. But true leadership, born of Nobility, requires no proclamations or grand gestures. It is quiet yet unmistakable, as it carries the weight of integrity, the depth of self-respect, and the grace of a man who embodies his highest self.

Ultimately, the foundation of Nobility is self-respect. How we view ourselves directly shapes how others perceive us. A man who respects himself—who honors his values, cultivates his virtues, and lives with purpose—naturally commands the respect of others. Nobility is, therefore, not something we seek from the outside; it is something we cultivate from within, and in doing so, we create a presence that inspires and elevates all those around us.

Nobility, as a virtue, shines brightest when it is expressed through action. It is not a theoretical ideal or a distant aspiration but a quality that comes to life in the choices we make and the way we conduct ourselves every day. While the essence of Nobility is rooted within, its power is revealed through how we show up in the world, particularly in moments of adversity, service, and relationship.

A noble man's actions are defined by restraint, respect, and generosity. Restraint is not weakness but strength under control. It is the ability to pause, consider, and act with intention rather than react impulsively. In heated situations, a noble man remains composed, refusing to let his emotions or ego dictate his behavior. This restraint elevates the tone of interactions, fostering mutual respect and paving the way for solutions rooted in wisdom and understanding.

Respect is the cornerstone of all noble actions. A man of Nobility treats everyone—from the highest to the humblest—with dignity and consideration. He listens attentively, speaks kindly, and honors the humanity in others, even when they fail to see it in themselves. This respect extends beyond people to encompass all of life, including nature, traditions, and the delicate balance of the world around him.

Generosity, in the context of Nobility, goes beyond material giving. It is the willingness to give of oneself—to share time, energy, and attention in service to others. A noble man seeks to uplift and inspire those around him, not for recognition or reward but because it is simply who he is. His presence becomes a gift, creating an atmosphere of trust, harmony, and goodwill.

The true test of Nobility often comes in adversity. When faced with challenges, a noble man does not falter or descend into blame, anger, or bitterness. Instead, he rises, meeting difficulty with courage, composure, and a steadfast commitment to his principles. He does not shy away from responsibility or difficult decisions, knowing that his actions in such moments set the tone for others. In adversity, Nobility acts as a guiding light, elevating the situation and those involved.

In relationships, Nobility creates a foundation of trust and safety. A noble man shows up fully, offering his presence, honesty, and unwavering support. He sees and values the people in his life, creating a space where they feel deeply respected and cherished. This is particularly powerful in his relationships with the Feminine, where his Nobility allows him to hold space for vulnerability and depth, fostering connection on the Soul level. The Feminine, attuned to the energetic subtleties of life, intuitively recognizes and responds to Nobility. It is felt in the way he listens, the steadiness of his presence, and the care in his actions.

The ripple effect of Nobility cannot be overstated. When a man embodies this virtue, it inspires and elevates everyone around him. His restraint diffuses conflict; his respect fosters mutual understanding; his generosity creates bonds of goodwill. A noble man does not seek to dominate or control but to lead by example, quietly but powerfully transforming the environment around him.

Through Nobility in action, a man becomes more than just a participant in life—he becomes a creator of harmony and trust. This is where the true power of Nobility lies: in its ability to bring out the best in others, to create spaces where growth and connection flourish, and to leave a legacy of integrity and respect. Nobility, in action, becomes the bridge between the man we are and the man we aspire to be.

Nobility is not only a quality of character; it is a pathway to our higher self and a deeper connection with the Divine. At its core, Nobility is an expression of alignment—with universal principles, natural laws, and the eternal wisdom that flows through all of creation. To embody Nobility is to live in harmony with this higher order, rising above ego-driven desires and embracing a life of service and meaning.

A noble man recognizes that his actions, thoughts, and words ripple outward, shaping not only his immediate environment but also the web of consciousness that connects all beings. This awareness instills a profound sense of responsibility, not as a burden but as a calling. The noble man understands that by serving a greater good, he serves himself in the highest sense—aligning his temporal existence with the infinite purpose of his Soul.

Being in service to the greater good is a hallmark of Nobility, but it is not servitude. It is an offering of one's strength, wisdom, and compassion to uplift others, not for recognition or validation but because it is simply the right thing to do. This service enriches the noble man as much as it benefits those he touches. It nourishes his Soul and creates a magnetic quality that naturally draws respect, trust, and admiration from others.

This connection to the Divine and the higher self imbues Nobility with a quiet power. It is not the power of dominance or control but the power of presence and integrity. A noble man stands as a beacon, his essence radiating trust, safety, and inspiration. The Feminine, in particular, feels this quality deeply, as Nobility provides the fertile ground for trust, openness, and surrender in any relationship.

By anchoring himself in his higher self, the noble man becomes a custodian of harmony and beauty in the world. His life becomes a reflection of the Divine principles he embodies, inspiring others to rise and follow his example. Nobility, then, is not just a virtue; it is a bridge between the earthly and the eternal, guiding us to live a life of depth, meaning, and grace.

Nobility is not a lofty ideal reserved for moments of grandeur—it is lived and demonstrated in the smallest daily choices. It begins with inner alignment: the integrity of our thoughts and the clarity of our intentions. A noble man first cultivates Nobility within, ensuring that his internal world is one of coherence, truth, and dignity. Only then can his outer actions authentically reflect this quality.

In practice, Nobility shows up in how we speak, act, and treat others. It is the choice to speak with kindness, even when we are met with hostility. It is the decision to act with fairness and generosity, even when doing so is inconvenient. It is the discipline to honor our commitments and the humility to admit when we fall short. Most importantly, Nobility requires us to be conscious of our thoughts, as they shape how we perceive and engage with the world.

In relationships, Nobility fosters trust and safety, especially with the Feminine. When a man embodies Nobility, he provides a container of presence and respect that allows others to feel valued and seen. This is not achieved through grand gestures but through consistent, thoughtful actions that demonstrate depth of character. A noble man lifts those around him, not by overpowering but by empowering.

The practice of Nobility is an ongoing commitment. Each choice, no matter how small, becomes an opportunity to embody this virtue and to bring a higher standard of conduct into the world.

In a world that increasingly idolizes the superficial and fleeting, the need for noble men has never been greater. The exalted Masculine archetype is a rare and precious counterbalance to a culture that often celebrates the shallow over the substantive. Nobility, with its quiet power and dignified presence, offers a way to heal and elevate the fractured fabric of our society.

Chivalry, once a hallmark of manhood, has been largely forgotten, replaced by pursuits of dominance, materialism, and empty bravado. Yet, the noble man redefines what it means to lead and inspire. He embodies majesty without arrogance, strength without oppression, and confidence without bravado. He becomes a *"gentle man"* in the truest sense: gentle in his demeanor, firm in his principles, and unwavering in his service to the greater good.

To embody Nobility is to accept the sacred duty to elevate all you touch. It is a daily practice, an act of quiet revolution, and a choice to stand as a beacon of what is possible. The world does not need more loud voices—it needs more noble ones.

The question is: Will you answer the call?

Once you see, you cannot unsee.

PRACTICE MAKES PERFECT,
MASTERY IS EARNED

VIRTUE #7: NOBILITY

Exercise: Embodying Nobility in Daily Life

This exercise is designed to help you consciously culti-vate and embody Nobility in your thoughts, actions, and presence. Nobility, as a virtue, requires both self-aware-ness and intentional practice, and these three steps will guide you to integrate this virtue into your daily life.

Step 1: Reflect on Your Inner Alignment
Take five minutes at the start or end of your day to reflect on the state of your inner world. Ask yourself:

- Are my thoughts aligned with my highest values?
- Am I acting in a way that reflects my principles and character?
- Have I allowed fear, ego, or lower nature cravings to dictate my actions or responses today?

This self-inquiry helps you identify any dissonance between your inner alignment and outer actions. It's not about judgment but clarity. Use this reflection to reaffirm your commitment to living as a noble man, embodying integrity, majesty, and grace.

Step 2: Make Nobility a Conscious Choice

Throughout your day, intentionally bring Nobility into your interactions and decisions. Before responding to a challenge, engaging in conversation, or making a choice, pause and ask:

- Am I acting with dignity, respect, and grace?
- How can I elevate this situation for the highest good of all involved?
- What would a noble man do in this moment?

This practice requires mindfulness and a willingness to choose higher ground, even when it feels inconvenient or challenging. Each small act of Nobility strengthens your ability to embody this virtue.

Step 3: Observe the Ripple Effect

At the end of your day, take a moment to reflect on how your noble actions influenced others and your environment. Ask yourself:

- Did I notice any shifts in how others responded to me?
- How did embodying Nobility impact my own sense of peace and self-respect?
- What lessons did I learn about the power of Nobility today?

This step is about cultivating awareness of how your presence and actions create ripples in the world around you. Over time, you will see how embodying Nobility elevates not only your life but also the lives of those you touch.

Final Note

Nobility is not about perfection but about presence. It is a daily practice, an ongoing commitment to show up as the best version of yourself. Begin small, and let each noble choice build momentum as you continue to embody this exalted virtue.

DISCIPLINE

NOBODY HAS EVER SLACKED OR SLOTHED THEIR way to greatness. Whether in the material world or in spiritual ascension, no man has stumbled into mastery through laziness. Discipline is the keystone virtue that upholds Order and Integrity—the very bedrock of the exalted Masculine archetype. Without Discipline, all other virtues collapse under the weight of inaction.

Yet, in modern society, Discipline is often misunderstood. It is seen as restriction rather than freedom, as a burden rather than power. This is the lie of the lower nature—that comfort is the ultimate goal, that ease is preferable to effort. In truth, nothing enslaves a man more than his indulgence in laziness and unchecked desire. The undisciplined man is at the mercy of external forces, swayed by his emotions, dictated by his cravings, and ultimately trapped in mediocrity.

Sloth is not simply a lack of action—it is the active decay of a man's potential. It manifests as procrastination, excuse-making, avoidance, and passivity. And while many men believe they are avoiding discomfort, they are, in fact, welcoming a greater suffering—the suffering of stagnation. A man without Discipline is like a blade left unsharpened, dull and ineffective when the moment of challenge arrives.

Contrast this with the disciplined man. He is not enslaved by fleeting desires but governed by a higher order of self-command. His actions are intentional, his mind is sharp, and his presence exudes power. He does not waste his days in idle comforts but tempers himself like steel in the fire of consistent effort. His Discipline is not just a habit—it is a declaration of who he is.

The exalted Masculine does not tolerate sloth in himself. He understands that to be undisciplined is to be dishonorable—to himself, his potential, and those who depend on him. He knows that where there is no Discipline, there is no true Order, and where there is no Order, chaos reigns.

The question is simple: Who owns who? Does a man own his impulses, or do his impulses own him? That is the defining difference between the man who lives in sovereignty and the man who lives as a slave to circumstance.

Arguably, the first step toward power, mastery, and true freedom begins with Discipline.

A spiritual mentor once told me: "Unless your spirituality changes the way you do the dishes, you haven't advanced much yet."

At the time, I didn't grasp the depth of this statement. What do spirituality and doing the dishes have in common? Wasn't Discipline reserved for grand pursuits—building businesses, training the body, mastering the mind? What did something as mundane as scrubbing a plate have to do with the path of an exalted man?

But in time, I came to understand: Discipline is not just about doing—it is about *Being*.

A man's Discipline is revealed in the smallest, most ordinary aspects of his life. His kitchen, his workspace, his car, his grooming, his posture, his words. All of these are reflections of his inner state. The way he moves through the world and the way he engages with each task—whether sweeping a floor or leading a company—is a direct expression of his integrity and presence.

Sloth is a lack of presence. It is moving through life on autopilot, engaging with the world passively, without care or attention. When we do something half-heartedly, without precision or presence, we are not truly engaged with Life itself. And the man who is not engaged with Life cannot claim to be in mastery of it.

Contrast this with a man of Discipline. When he speaks, he speaks with clarity and intention. When he trains, he trains with purpose. When he works, he works with excellence. When he rests, he rests fully. He does not drift aimlessly through his days—he inhabits them fully, with vigor.

This is why Discipline is the bridge between action and mastery. It is not about perfectionism or obsession; it is about bringing full awareness into all that we do.

The exalted Masculine does not tolerate mediocrity in himself. He understands that excellence is not an outcome—it is a habit, a way of *Being*. Aristotle said it best: "We are what we repeatedly do. Excellence, then, is not an act but a habit."

This means that Discipline is not about occasional heroic efforts but about the daily, consistent choices we make. It is in the seemingly insignificant acts—how we carry ourselves, how we follow through, how we meet each moment with presence— that a man of depth and character is forged.

Discipline is not punishment. It is an act of devotion—to oneself, to one's purpose, and to the sacred responsibility of living as a fully actualized man.

Sloth is passive, but vigor is active. A man who is alive in his body, mind, and spirit brings a force of vitality into everything he touches. This vigor is not just energy—it is deliberate engagement with life. It is how a man turns mere effort into momentum, and he turns momentum into mastery.

Vigor is not about brute force or constant exertion. It is about the intensity of presence we bring to each moment. When we are truly present, we energize what we engage with—we infuse it with Life itself. Whether it is our work, our training, our relationships, or our creative pursuits, what we give our full attention and effort to naturally flourishes.

The undisciplined man lacks vigor not because he is incapable, but because he has allowed himself to slip into passivity. He drifts, waiting for motivation to strike instead of acting in spite of how he feels. He hesitates, hoping for the perfect conditions before moving forward, not realizing that action creates the very energy he lacks.

Discipline, then, is not just about consistency—it is about how we show up. It is not enough to merely go through the motions; we must imbue our actions with meaning and intent. This is how vigor becomes the catalyst for greatness.

Think of a man chopping wood. The slothful man swings his axe mindlessly, distracted, weak in his stroke. He will tire quickly, achieving little. The disciplined man, however, brings his full awareness to each swing—his stance, his grip, the arc of the blade. Each strike lands cleanly, efficiently, powerfully. He does more with less effort because he is fully engaged.

This is the secret: When we cultivate vigor in all we do, we unlock efficiency, precision, and impact. Life ceases to feel like an uphill battle because we are no longer leaking energy through distraction and half-hearted effort.

A man who embodies the exalted Masculine does not dabble. He does not live life lukewarm, hesitating between action and inaction. He moves with purpose—and because of this, his presence alone commands respect.

This is why vigor is inseparable from true Discipline. Vigor gives Discipline power—it turns routine into ritual, duty into devotion, and effort into mastery. Without it, Discipline risks becoming rigid and mechanical. With it, Discipline becomes a force of nature—alive, fluid, and unwavering.

The greatest leaders, warriors, and sages in history did not just do—*they did with fire*. Their Discipline was infused with spirit, their actions brimming with intent and vitality. This is the energy of the noble man.

So, how do we cultivate vigor? Through choice.

Vigor is a decision. A choice to bring full energy and engagement to whatever we do.

We begin in small ways. We make our bed with care. We train our body with purpose. We complete our work with full attention. We hold our posture with presence. We speak with clarity. We listen with depth.

We practice this until it becomes a way of *Being*. And soon, we no longer have to "try" to be disciplined—Discipline becomes who we are.

At first glance, Discipline may seem like the opposite of freedom—rules, structure, and restraint instead of spontaneity, ease, and pleasure. But this is an illusion. True freedom is not found in the absence of structure, but in the mastery of it.

A man without Discipline is not free. He is enslaved to his impulses, his emotions, his distractions, and his weaknesses. He does not decide his actions; they are dictated by external forces or fleeting desires. He is at the mercy of his environment rather than the architect of his destiny.

Discipline is the gateway to sovereignty.

A man who masters himself—his body, mind, and actions—is unshackled from the chains that bind lesser men. He is free to pursue his highest calling, not because he is lucky, but because he has forged the will to do so.

This is why Discipline is a keystone of the exalted Masculine. It builds upon Order and Integrity—without it, these virtues remain abstract ideals rather than lived realities.

- Order requires Discipline to be maintained. Without it, Order collapses into chaos.
- Integrity requires Discipline to be upheld. Without it, Integrity becomes situational rather than unwavering.

Discipline is the force that solidifies a man's code, making it unbreakable. It ensures that his principles are not just words but a way of life.

Men who lack Discipline are easily swayed, controlled, or manipulated. They have no foundation of their own—they move in whichever direction their cravings or circumstances push them.

But the disciplined man is grounded. He cannot be tempted off his path by cheap pleasures or easy distractions. He does not allow emotions to override his principles. He has cultivated the strength to choose the hard right over the easy wrong.

This inner fortitude is the source of all great power. It is what allows a man to build, protect, lead, and elevate. It is why great warriors, leaders, and philosophers alike have revered Discipline as a sacred virtue.

The undisciplined man looks at the disciplined man and thinks, "He must be miserable, constantly restraining himself." But the reality is the opposite. The disciplined man moves through life with greater ease, greater clarity, and greater strength.

He does not waste energy on regret, indecision, or self-sabotage. His path is clear because he has chosen it.

The reward for this commitment? Freedom.

- Freedom from the tyranny of cravings.
- Freedom from the chaos of a disordered mind.
- Freedom from the weakness that breeds regret.

Discipline is not a burden—it is the great liberator.

Once you see, you cannot unsee.

PRACTICE MAKES PERFECT, MASTERY IS EARNED

VIRTUE #8: DISCIPLINE

Mastering the Self: Cultivating Discipline as a Daily Practice

Discipline is not something we either have or don't have—it is a muscle that grows stronger with use. The key to developing Discipline is conscious, consistent practice in small, manageable ways that compound over time.

This exercise is designed to help the reader do three things: become aware of where they lack Discipline, develop a simple system to strengthen it, and integrate it into their daily life.

Step 1: Identify the Gaps (Self-Awareness & Ownership)
- Take a moment to reflect on your life.
- Identify **one** area where a **lack of Discipline is limiting your potential.** This could be physical (fitness, diet, sleep), mental (focus, study, reading), emotional (reactivity, patience, relationships), or spiritual (meditation, presence, devotion).
- **Write it down.** Be specific. Example: "I lack the Discipline to wake up early and stick to a morning routine."

Key Insight: Self-mastery starts with radical honesty. You cannot fix what you refuse to acknowledge.

Step 2: Implement the Rule of One (Simplicity & Consistency)

- Select **one small, non-negotiable action** to strengthen your Discipline in that area.
- Keep it **simple** and **realistic** but meaningful. Example: "For the next 7 days, I will wake up at 6 AM and start my morning routine with 10 minutes of stretching and breathing."
- **Commit to it for one week—no excuses.**

Key Insight: Many men fail at Discipline because they take on too much at once. Mastery begins with **one small but powerful step**, consistently applied.

Step 3: Own the Outcome (Reflection & Expansion)

- At the end of the week, **review your progress**. Did you keep your commitment? How did it impact your mindset, energy, and productivity?
- If you completed the challenge, **expand it**. Example: "Now, I will extend my morning routine to 30 minutes."
- If you fell short, **analyze why without judgment**. Adjust and **restart immediately**— Discipline is built through resilience, not perfection.

Key Insight: Discipline is not about getting it perfect—it's about showing up consistently, adjusting, and expanding.

Final Note

Discipline is not something you "find." It is something you **create**. Every time you choose to **follow through, even when it's hard, you strengthen the foundation of your character**.

Now, **begin**. The path of the exalted Masculine is forged through action.

VIRTUE #9
VALOR

V ALOR IS OFTEN MISTAKEN FOR MERE COURAGE, but it is something far greater. Courage alone is the willingness to act in the face of fear, but Valor is courage imbued with heroism, honor, and an unwavering commitment to a higher cause. It is the mark of the spiritual warrior—one who faces not just the dangers of the external world but also the battles waged within his own Soul.

A man of Valor does not simply endure; he charges forward despite uncertainty, despite risk, and despite the overwhelming odds stacked against him. He is not reckless, but neither is he ruled by fear. He understands that fear is a natural response, but he refuses to bow to it. Instead, he alchemizes fear into fuel, transforming it into clarity, focus, and unshakable resolve.

True Valor is not about the absence of fear but the mastery of it. It is not about reckless defiance but a deeply rooted sense of purpose that makes action inevitable, even when it is difficult, painful, or seemingly impossible. It is the exalted Masculine standing firm in the face of the unknown, undeterred by failure, and wholly committed to the journey ahead.

THE NOBLE WARRIOR'S INNER BATTLE

While Valor is often associated with battlefield heroics, its deepest expression is found in the unseen battles within. The greatest adversaries a man will ever face are not found in the outside world but within his own mind. Fear, doubt, insecurity, self-sabotage, and the gnawing belief that he is not enough—these are the dragons he must slay.

For most men, these inner adversaries are far more crippling than any external foe. The fear of failure, the paralysis of indecision, the weight of expectation—these can keep a man shackled in mediocrity, playing small in a life that craves him to play big.

But the man of Valor knows that failure is not a reflection of his worth; it is simply the tuition he must pay for his growth. He understands that to avoid failure is to avoid Life itself. Valor calls him to step forward, to embrace the trials, and to face his fears head-on, knowing that every challenge, every defeat, and every hard-won victory is forging him into something greater.

The warrior does not seek comfort; he seeks conquest—not of others, but of himself. He knows that the greatest triumph is mastery over his own fears, and he is willing to enter and face that battle every single day.

THE FOUNDATIONS OF VALOR

Valor is not the absence of fear—it is mastery over it. Fear is a fundamental part of the human experience, embedded deep in our psyche as a survival mechanism. But when left unchecked, it mutates into a force that controls us, shaping our choices, dictating our actions, and keeping us small. The exalted Masculine does not seek to eliminate fear; he seeks to confront, integrate, and rise above it.

Fear whispers insidiously in the shadowy corners of our Mind, masquerading as logic, prudence, or self-preservation. It tells us to stay where it is safe, to avoid risk, to not dare too greatly. Yet, when we submit to this voice, we unknowingly surrender to the slow decay of our own potential. True Valor is not reckless—it is the calculated decision to move forward despite fear, guided by wisdom, courage, and the unwavering belief in one's purpose.

Bravery in the exalted Masculine is twofold. It manifests outwardly in moments of external crisis—when a man must defend, protect, or rise to the occasion. But just as importantly, it manifests inwardly in the silent battles he fights within himself. The battle against self-doubt. The battle against the fear of failure. The battle against resignation, cynicism, and the urge to remain in comfortable mediocrity.

The noble warrior understands that failure is not his enemy—stagnation is. Every man who has ever achieved anything of true significance has met failure countless times along the way. But he refuses to identify with his failures, knowing that they do not define him. Instead, he harnesses them as stepping stones to greatness. A man of Valor knows that the only true failure is failing to try, failing to dare, failing to step into the unknown with faith in his own capacity to prevail.

This is the spirit of the warrior. The man who embraces Valor sees that life itself is a battleground—not a war fought against others but a proving ground for his own strength, resilience, and unwavering will to grow, expand, and evolve. He does not retreat in the face of adversity; he leans in. He does not break under pressure; he transforms. He does not cower before the unknown; he meets it with an unshakable heart.

Valor, then, is not just about momentary acts of bravery—it is a way of *Being*. It is a quiet decision, made day after day, to step forward in defiance of fear, to act in accordance with one's highest ideals, and to embrace every challenge as an initiation into a greater version of oneself.

VALOR IN ACTION

Valor is not merely a virtue spoken about in grand philosophical terms—it is lived. It is revealed in the way a man stands, speaks, and moves through life. It is in the small, daily choices he makes just as much as in the defining moments of his existence. Valor is not something he claims for himself; it is something the world recognizes in him because of how he shows up.

A man of Valor does not flinch in the face of adversity. When life presents obstacles, he does not recoil, complain, or seek escape. He meets challenges head-on, understanding that difficulty is not an affliction—it is an initiation. The hardships he encounters are not punishments; they are the very forge that tempers his steel. He does not ask for a lighter burden—he seeks to build, expand, and evolve his capacity to carry it.

This same courage extends beyond the external battlefield into the internal one. The noble warrior confronts his fears, doubts, and insecurities with the same boldness he would display against any external adversary. When his Mind fills with uncertainty, he does not succumb to paralysis. When his confidence wavers, he does not retreat into self-pity. When he falls, he does not wallow in despair—he rises, again and again.

Valor is also the refusal to be swayed by the expectations or judgments of others. The exalted Masculine understands that society will often misunderstand and resist men of true courage. The masses may ridicule him, dismiss him, or attempt to bring him down to their level of complacency. But he does not seek approval—he seeks Truth. His own Truth more so than the Truth of others, and the Truth about Life itself more so than his own Truth. He does not bend his principles for acceptance; he stands firm in his convictions.

The man of Valor does not wait for the perfect conditions to act. He does not hesitate, hoping for more clarity, more certainty, or more reassurance. He knows that the moment to act is now. He trusts himself. He moves forward with decisiveness. His path is not always clear, but he knows what's in his Heart and won't let his Mind obscure or override this North Star, and that is enough to press forward into the unknown and unfamiliar.

True Valor is not about bravado or seeking recognition. It does not demand applause, nor does it even require an audience. The most profound acts of courage are often those that go unseen— the silent fire walks waged in the depths of his Soul. Choosing to forgive when vengeance would be easier. Speaking Truth when silence would be safer. Standing alone when the crowd moves in a different direction.

Ultimately, Valor is not about victory or defeat—it is about the will to walk the fire, the resolve to stand firm, and the indomitable spirit that refuses to be conquered by his lower nature fears and dragons. A man of Valor understands that, in the end, the greatest conquests are not won on the battlefield of the Outer World but within the chambers of his own Heart. And there, in that sacred place, he wages the only conquest that truly matters—the mastery and illumination of his own Soul.

THE INNER BATTLEFIELD
Overcoming the Fear of Failure

A man of Valor does not seek to avoid failure—he embraces it as part of his path. He understands that failure is not an indictment of his worth nor a verdict on his destiny. It is merely a teacher, a forge that refines his will, his skill, and his spirit. The weak man is paralyzed by the fear of failing, mistaking every misstep as proof of his inadequacy. The man of Valor, however, knows that failure is not his enemy—it is his mentor.

At the root of this fear is the false and highly limiting belief that failing at something must mean that we are a failure. This insidious misconception keeps men bound in hesitation, afraid to risk, afraid to leap, afraid to truly live. But the exalted Masculine knows better—he recognizes that failure is, at best, an imposter and not the opposite of success but its most faithful companion. Every great warrior, every legendary leader, every enlightened sage has faced defeat and disappointment. What set them apart was not their avoidance of failure but their refusal to be defined by it.

Valor means stepping forward despite the possibility of failure. It means taking risks, knowing that setbacks are not indicators to retreat but invitations to refine. It means committing fully to the pursuit of something greater than oneself, undeterred by the prospect of stumbling along the way. The only true failure is inaction toward our dreams and desires—the choice to remain idle out of fear.

To embody Valor is to reframe failure, to see it not as a finality but as a step toward mastery. Every stumble is a lesson. Every mistake is an opportunity to sharpen awareness. Every setback is a test of resilience. A man of Valor does not lament his losses, nor does he ignore them—he studies them. He extracts wisdom from every misstep and uses it to fuel his evolution.

Moreover, he refuses to let past failures dictate his future. He does not carry the weight of his past as a burden; he wields it as a weapon. Every scar is a mark of experience, every wound a lesson written into the fabric of his Soul. He does not shrink from challenges because of what has gone wrong before—he faces them with renewed strength, knowing that he has already endured and risen.

Valor is the art of moving forward in the face of uncertainty. It is the willingness to try, to risk, to strive for greatness, knowing that the only thing worse than failing is the regret of never having dared at all. A man who embraces failure as part of his journey will, in time, rise above it and transform into something far greater than he ever imagined. He will no longer fear falling, for he knows how to rise.

THE CALL TO HEROISM
The Spiritual Warrior's Path

Valor is not simply about courage in the face of external threats—it is the daily choice to rise above one's inner adversaries. The greatest battles a man will ever fight are not against armies or opponents but against his own fears, doubts, and limitations. These are the invisible enemies that seek to erode his will, to keep him small, to whisper to him that he is not enough. A man of Valor knows that his path is one of continuous battle—not against the world, but against the lesser version of himself.

The world often speaks of heroism in grand terms—warriors on battlefields, men who run into burning buildings, and those who face mortal danger for the sake of others. These are indeed acts of undeniable bravery, but heroism does not always wear armor or wield a sword. True heroism is found in the silent, unseen moments of a man's life—the moment he chooses to stand by his principles when it is easier to fold, the moment he refuses to let fear dictate his choices, the moment he steps into the unknown with faith instead of retreating into comfort.

The exalted Masculine understands that the highest expression of Valor is not reckless bravado nor the absence of fear but the willingness to act despite fear. He does not need the world's applause to confirm his bravery—he walks his path with quiet certainty, knowing that his greatest victories are won in the inner sanctum of his own Soul. He knows that every moment of hesitation, every excuse, every rationalization is an enemy in disguise, luring him into complacency. The weak man succumbs to these illusions. The man of Valor wields his will as a blade, cutting through all barriers with clarity and purpose.

To walk the spiritual warrior's path is to embrace discomfort and to recognize that true growth lies beyond the edges of what is safe and known. It means willingly stepping into the fire of hardship, knowing that it is through trial that strength is forged. It means holding oneself to a higher standard—not because the world demands it, but because one's own Soul does. The noble warrior does not seek battle and conquest for its own sake, but when faced with a worthy challenge—be it external or internal—he does not flinch.

Valor demands sacrifice. It requires that a man surrender the false comforts of self-doubt, procrastination, and indecision. It demands that he let go of the stories that keep him small, that he relinquish the illusion that life will one day be without risk. The man of Valor does not wait for the perfect moment, the perfect plan, the perfect conditions—he moves forward despite the uncertainty, knowing that action itself is the bridge between fear and triumph.

The spiritual warrior's path is not for the faint-hearted. It is not for those who wish to be coddled by ease and mediocrity. It is for those who are willing to face themselves with honesty, to meet their weaknesses with resolve, and to step into the arena of life fully engaged. The battle is never truly won, for every victory opens the door to the next challenge. But the man of Valor does not seek an end to the conquest—he seeks to become the kind of man who can meet each of Life's inevitable trials and challenges with unwavering strength, relentless courage, and a Heart that will not yield.

This is the way of the exalted Masculine. This is the path of the noble warrior. This is Valor.

Once you see, you cannot unsee.

PRACTICE MAKES PERFECT,
MASTERY IS EARNED

VIRTUE #9: VALOR

Exercise: Stepping into the Arena of Valor

This exercise is designed to help you confront and move beyond the fears, doubts, and internal obstacles that hold you back. By taking decisive action in the face of resistance, you cultivate the virtue of Valor—the mark of a noble warrior who does not shrink from challenge but rises to meet it.

Step 1: Identify Your Inner Adversary
Take a moment to reflect on where fear, doubt, or hesitation holds you back. This could be in any area of life—your career, relationships, personal growth, or a specific challenge you've been avoiding. Ask yourself:
  • What is one thing I deeply desire to do but have been avoiding out of fear?
  • What inner voice or story is keeping me from taking action?
  • If I do not face this, what will be the long-term consequence?
Write down your answers. Be brutally honest. Name your adversary—whether it is fear of failure, fear of rejection, self-doubt, or a limiting belief you've carried for too long.

Step 2: Choose the Spiritual Warrior's Path

Now that you've identified your inner adversary, commit to stepping forward despite the discomfort. Take a deep breath and visualize yourself standing at the threshold of battle—not against an external enemy, but against the limitations within you.

- What is one courageous action I can take today— right now—to move past this fear?
- If I knew that failure was just another step toward mastery, what would I do differently?
- How would the man of Valor within me respond to this challenge?

Write down the action you will take immediately. The key is not to overthink but to act. Valor is forged in action, not contemplation.

Step 3: Enter the Arena and Reflect

Now, take that action—no matter how small. It could be making the phone call you've been dreading, speaking your truth in a difficult conversation, stepping into a challenging situation with confidence, or simply deciding that fear will no longer dictate your life.

Once you have taken action, reflect:
- What did I feel before taking action?
- What did I feel after taking action?
- How can I make courageous action a habit in my daily life?

Write down your reflections. Notice how fear loses its power when confronted directly. The more you step into

the arena of Valor, the more you will embody the noble
warrior within.

Final Thought
Every act of courage, no matter how small, strengthens
the muscle of Valor. The warrior does not wait for the
absence of fear—he moves forward in its presence. This
is your path. Walk it with strength.

VIRTUE #10

FORTITUDE

FORTITUDE IS THE BEDROCK OF THE EXALTED Masculine archetype—the unwavering inner strength that allows a man to stand resolute, unshaken by the storms of Life. It is not mere toughness, nor is it simply perseverance. It is something deeper, something more elemental. Fortitude is the fire that burns within, the force that refuses to collapse in the face of adversity, the knowing that no matter what comes, you will endure—not merely surviving, but transcending.

Unlike Valor, which draws on our reservoir of courage to overcome such imposters as fear, doubt, limiting beliefs, and other inner dragons and outer trials and challenges, Fortitude is the steady foundation upon which a man builds his existence. It is not flashy and often comes without the bravery and heroism we might find in Valor. Fortitude simply does not seek recognition. Fortitude is the quiet, relentless force that allows a man to keep going long after others have given up. It is what holds Order when Chaos attempts to overwhelm. It is what remains standing when everything else has fallen or collapsed.

In its essence, Fortitude is the ability to hold one's center, to remain anchored in Truth, even in the face of hardship, uncertainty, or prolonged struggle. It is not about brute force or defying difficulty for the sake of it; rather, it is about having the depth of character, the internal resilience, and the spiritual endurance to walk your path no matter how difficult the terrain.

Most importantly, Fortitude is what allows a man to stay aligned with his Higher Self when Life tests him. And Life will test him. Every man will face moments when his strength, his faith, his very essence will be challenged. The difference between those who break and those who transcend is Fortitude.

But what is the nature of this inner strength? It is not aggression, nor is it emotional suppression. True Fortitude is a dynamic interplay between resilience and surrender—an acceptance of hardship not as a burden but as a forge. Fortitude does not resist Life; it absorbs the blows, integrates the lessons, and emerges stronger, clearer, and more deeply rooted.

This is why Fortitude is not just a practical necessity—it is a spiritual imperative. A man of Fortitude is not merely a strong man; he is a man who cannot be owned by fear, doubt, or hardship. He is a man who stands firm in his path, not because he has never faltered, but because he has fallen, risen, and come to understand that true strength is found in one's willingness to keep walking forward, no matter what.

Fortitude is the quiet vow you make with yourself: I might get destroyed from time to time, but I will not get defeated.

Fortitude is not something a man is born with; it is something he builds, brick by brick, through trial, hardship, and relentless perseverance. It is a virtue forged in the fire of experience, strengthened through struggle, and polished by wisdom. Fortitude is cultivated, not gifted, and like any profound inner strength, it must be earned through living.

And in this, Fortitude becomes the great equalizer among men. Wealth, privilege, or status cannot bestow it upon you, nor can inherited advantages shield a man from the trials necessary to forge it. The man born into hardship has just as much access to Fortitude as the one born with a silver spoon in his mouth—perhaps even more so, as struggle is the anvil upon which Fortitude is hammered into shape. No man is exempt from the tests of Life, and no man can buy, inherit, or fake the unwavering resilience that only comes through standing in the fire and refusing to be consumed by it.

At its core, Fortitude is the unbreakable alignment between a man's will and his deeper Truth. This is what makes it different from sheer willpower or stubbornness. Fortitude is not about forcing or overpowering Life; rather, it is about standing firmly within oneself, regardless of the challenges, setbacks, or suffering one must endure. A man of Fortitude does not flinch, does not retreat, does not surrender his integrity when Life tests him.

The foundation of Fortitude rests upon three key pillars:

1. **Endurance Through Adversity**—Fortitude is the ability to withstand hardship, suffering, and difficulty without breaking. It is the power to persist when everything within and around you screams for surrender. This is not simply physical endurance, though that is a byproduct—it is a deep, unwavering spiritual resilience. A man of Fortitude does not crumble under pressure; he holds his ground, knowing that adversity is the crucible that refines his strength. Fortitude is the virtue that keeps a man standing when all else has fallen.

2. **Mastery over Softness**—Fortitude demands that a man rise above the temptations of ease, indulgence, and escape. Softness is the great corrupter—it whispers for comfort, encourages complacency, and lures men into the seductive trap of convenience, gluttony, and debauchery. A man ruled by softness indulges every craving, shirks discomfort, and resists nothing. Fortitude is the force that rejects this decay, forging a man into something solid and unshakable. It is the capacity to say *no* to excess, *yes* to challenge, and to cultivate the discipline that hardens both will and spirit. A man who has mastered Fortitude is not swayed by urges or enslaved by pleasure—he owns himself fully.

3. **Faith in Something Greater**—The highest expression
   of Fortitude is the ability to stand firm in the face of
   the unknown, trusting in something beyond oneself.
   Whether it is faith in God, the Universe, the Divine
   Order, or simply in one's own destiny, Fortitude allows
   a man to move forward without needing to see the
   entire path ahead. It is the spiritual anchor that prevents
   him from being tossed by the storms of doubt, fear,
   and uncertainty. A man of Fortitude does not need
   guarantees—he moves with faith, knowing that each
   step forward will reveal the next.

THE SILENT POWER OF FORTITUDE

Fortitude does not announce itself. It does not demand recognition, nor does it seek validation. It is the silent, steady inner force that enables a man to remain composed, unwavering, and resolute in the face of challenge. Unlike valor, which is often displayed in moments of crisis, Fortitude is a slow-burning fire—it is the day-in, day-out discipline of staying the course, showing up, and doing what must be done.

A man with Fortitude does not flinch at hardship, nor does he indulge in self-pity. He understands that suffering is not an aberration but an inevitability in life. He does not seek escape or wish for an easier path—he fortifies himself and walks through the storm. It is this quiet endurance, this ability to hold his ground without the need for applause or acknowledgment, that makes Fortitude one of the most defining virtues of the exalted Masculine.

It is also what makes Fortitude a rare and precious trait in today's world. In a period of instant gratification and external validation, where men are conditioned to seek comfort at all costs, Fortitude stands as a stark contrast. It is the trait that keeps a man steady when others crumble, the force that allows him to carry burdens without complaint, and the discipline that prevents him from wavering when lesser men fold.

True power is not loud. It does not posture, flex, or seek attention. It is silent, grounded, and immovable. This is the texture and tapestry of Fortitude.

FORTITUDE AND THE
REFINEMENT OF CHARACTER

Fortitude is the chisel that sculpts a man's character, shaping him through trials and perseverance. It is not granted but earned— refined through hardship, discipline, and unwavering commitment. A man's true nature is not revealed in comfort but in how he endures and overcomes.

Adversity is the forge, and Fortitude is the fire that hardens his will. It does not break him; it tempers him. Each time he chooses discipline over indulgence, commitment over convenience, and perseverance over surrender, he strengthens his foundation.

A refined man moves through life with an unshakable presence. He does not waver when others doubt him, nor does he bend to a world that rewards weakness. His strength is not loud; it does not need to be. It is evident in his presence, his words, and the quiet confidence that commands respect without force.

Fortitude, then, is not just about survival—it is about refinement. It is about emerging from life's crucible as a man of depth, resilience, and unshakable character.

FORTITUDE IN RELATIONSHIPS AND BROTHERHOOD

A man of Fortitude does not walk alone. Strength is not isolation—it is the ability to stand firm while also lifting others. In relationships, Fortitude manifests as unwavering integrity, the ability to hold space, and the resilience to navigate conflict without crumbling under pressure.

A man without Fortitude is easily swayed by emotion, external validation, or the need for approval. He avoids difficult conversations, betrays his own values to appease others, and shrinks in the face of adversity. The man of Fortitude, however, remains steady. He does not lash out in anger nor retreat into passivity. He meets challenges with resolve, offering clarity and stability to those around him.

In brotherhood, Fortitude is a bond forged in trust and tested through time. A man with Fortitude is someone others can rely on—his word is his oath, and his presence is a source of stability. He is the one that others turn to, not because he has all the answers but because he possesses the inner strength to stand firm when storms arise.

The exalted Masculine does not fear deep connection—he embraces it with strength and presence. He understands that true Fortitude is not about resisting vulnerability but carrying it with dignity, ensuring that he does not falter when those who rely on him need him most.

FORTITUDE IN ADVERSITY
The Crucible of Growth

What's likely becoming very clear by now is that Fortitude is not built in times of ease—it is forged in adversity. Hardship is not the enemy; it is the teacher. Every trial, setback, and moment of suffering is an invitation to strengthen our spirit, to deepen our resilience, and to prove to ourselves that we can endure, adapt, and overcome.

Without Fortitude, adversity breaks a man. He crumbles under pressure, succumbs to despair, or seeks escape in numbing distractions. He avoids challenges rather than meeting them head-on. But the man of Fortitude welcomes hardship, not because he enjoys suffering, but because he understands its purpose. He does not ask, *Why is this happening to me?* but rather, *What is this teaching me?*

This is the spiritual warrior's path—the ability to endure what others cannot, to rise when others fall, and to continue forward when all logic and comfort would demand surrender. The exalted Masculine does not just survive adversity; he is transformed by it. Each battle—whether internal or external—tempers him into something stronger, wiser, and more unwavering.

Adversity is inevitable. The question is, will it defeat us, or will we use its medicine to refine us? A man with Fortitude never lets hardship define him—he uses it to sharpen him into his highest expression.

FORTITUDE AS A DAILY PRACTICE
The Small Repetitions That Build an Unshakable Core

Paradoxically, Fortitude is more tested than built in life's grand challenges—it is mostly built and fortified through small, repeated acts in the seemingly mundane. It is easy to assume that inner strength is something we either have or don't, that it only emerges in times of great adversity. But in truth, Fortitude is a slow accumulation, formed in the ordinary moments of life, long before the storms arrive.

A man does not develop unshakable resolve by waiting for life's great tests to arrive. He forges it in the daily repetitions—waking up when he said he would, following through on commitments when no one is watching, and choosing integrity over convenience. He strengthens his will when he resists the urge to quit, when he holds the line against his lower nature, and when he does what is right even when it is uncomfortable.

These daily patterns carve deep neural grooves, creating a vast reservoir of resilience that will be there when life's inevitable trials arise. Without this conditioning, a man may find himself ill-equipped when a true test of spirit arrives. Fortitude is not something we summon only in the great trials and challenges we encounter along the way—it is something we live and breathe in the small, everyday moments, preparing us to stand firm when the ground beneath us begins to shake.

FORTITUDE AS AN ESSENCE VS. TRAIT

Fortitude is a virtue that a man carries within himself and leaves in his wake. It is the quiet force that allows him to navigate life's tempests with unshakable resolve, to endure without bitterness, and to rise time and again, no matter how many times he has been knocked down.

A man of Fortitude does not seek ease or comfort as his highest aim—he seeks the strength to bear what must be borne, to hold the line when others falter, and to act with integrity even when the cost is high. He does not break under pressure, nor does he seek to escape difficulty. Instead, he welcomes the weight of responsibility, knowing that through it, he is forged into something greater.

While there's a potent reinforcing interplay and connectedness between all the virtues, we could consider Fortitude as the rebar that reinforces and holds the whole foundation of all the virtues together. Without Fortitude, Discipline crumbles, Valor falters, and Nobility is hollow. It is the quiet engine that drives a man forward when his Mind tells him to stop, when his body begs for relief, and when the world offers him every excuse to quit.

Fortitude does not make a man invincible, but it does make him immovable. The storms of life will come—they are inevitable. But the man who has cultivated Fortitude will not merely endure; he will stand firm. He might bow and flex with the storms that come his way, but he will remain unbroken. And in doing so, he will not only uplift himself but also those who look to him for strength. Fortitude is not just something we embody for ourselves—it is a beacon that lights the way for others. The world needs men who will not retreat in the face of hardship, who will not complain about the weight of their burdens but instead carry them with honor.

Be that man.

Once you see, you cannot unsee.

PRACTICE MAKES PERFECT,
MASTERY IS EARNED

VIRTUE #10: FORTITUDE

Exercise: Building Your Fortitude Reservoir

The goal of this exercise is to take Fortitude beyond a mere concept or noble aspiration to being a lived experience—in other words, embodiment.

Step 1: Identify Your Daily Points of Resistance
Fortitude is not built in a single moment of extreme adversity but through daily choices. Start by identifying areas in your life where you tend to shrink, hesitate, or retreat when faced with discomfort. This could be avoiding difficult conversations, procrastinating on responsibilities, skipping workouts, or surrendering to mental doubts and insecurities.

- Write down three areas where you notice yourself resisting difficulty or taking the easy way out.
- Reflect on what thoughts, emotions, or fears accompany these moments of resistance.

Step 2: Lean Into Discomfort with Awareness
The key to cultivating Fortitude is choosing to embrace challenge rather than avoid it.

- Over the next week, deliberately engage in small acts of resilience. This could mean taking a cold shower, pushing yourself through the last rep at the gym, facing an uncomfortable conversation with courage, or saying *no* to an indulgence that weakens you.
- Each time you lean into discomfort, pause and acknowledge that this is an active *choice* to build Fortitude.
- Write a short reflection at the end of the day: How did it feel? What did you notice about your thoughts and emotions when you chose to persevere rather than retreat?

Step 3: Set a Fortitude Challenge

Building true Fortitude requires sustained commitment. Identify one challenge in your life that requires endurance, patience, or courage—something you've been avoiding or struggling with.

- Define a *Fortitude Challenge* for the next 30 days. This could be committing to a disciplined morning routine, quitting a bad habit, pushing through a difficult project, or training for something physically demanding.
- Track your progress daily. Each time you choose to persist, recognize it as an act of strengthening your inner foundation.

THE
SIDDHIS

"What are men? Mortal Gods.
What are Gods? Immortal men."

—HERACLITUS

SIDDHI EXPLAINED

THE SIDDHIS

A Gateway to Higher Consciousness

The term *siddhi* originates from ancient Sanskrit and is often translated as "attainment," "perfection," or "supernatural ability." In the yogic and spiritual traditions, Siddhis are extraordinary faculties that arise through deep spiritual practice, self-mastery, and alignment with higher consciousness. While many associate Siddhis with mystical powers—such as telepathy, levitation, or profound insight—these are merely symbolic representations of deeper inner qualities accessible to any man willing to walk the path of self-realization.

In the context of this Field Guide, the Siddhis are not merely reserved for sages or monks—they are tangible, embodied qualities that define the exalted Masculine archetype.

These are the subtle yet powerful attributes that govern a man's presence, depth, and ability to navigate the world with wisdom, integrity, and unwavering inner stability. They are not bestowed upon us from the outside; they are cultivated through intention, discipline, and devotion to the highest expression of our *Being*. Each Siddhi explored in this section—Awareness, Presence, Character, Worth, and Contentment—is a gateway to a more refined and powerful existence, enabling a man to move through life not just with strength but with an unmistakable radiance that comes from living in Truth.

Once you see, you cannot unsee.

AWARENESS

AWARENESS
The First Step to Mastery

AWARENESS IS THE FOUNDATION OF ALL TRANS-formation. Without it, a man is blind—blind to his own thoughts, emotions, and actions, blind to the impact he has on the world, and blind to the deeper reality that governs life beyond what his limited senses perceive. It is the difference between moving through life as a sovereign man, consciously shaping his existence, or drifting unconsciously, reacting to circumstances like a leaf caught in the wind.

But Awareness is not a binary switch—it is not something we either "have" or "lack." Rather, it is a spectrum, an ever-expanding aperture, much like the lens of a camera. A man with a narrow aperture of Awareness sees only what is directly in front of him—he is confined to the limits of his conditioning, personal biases, and habitual thinking. His world is small, his perspective is restricted, and his ability to grasp higher truths is obstructed.

As Awareness expands, so does a man's capacity to perceive reality in its depth and complexity. His aperture widens, allowing him to take in more light—more information, more intelligence, more truth. This is what we mean when we speak of ascending in consciousness or reaching a higher octave of Awareness. The more Aware we become, the more we begin to perceive the interwoven nature of all things, the hidden causes behind surface-level effects, and the underlying forces that shape our lives and the world at large.

Yet, Awareness is not merely about noticing more—it is about understanding at an increasingly sophisticated level. And here is where we must redefine intelligence. In the modern world, intelligence is often measured through academic performance, problem-solving skills, or raw cognitive ability—qualities that, while useful, do not necessarily produce wise or life-affirming outcomes. True intelligence, as defined by Natural Law, is "that which creates intelligent outcomes," and an intelligent outcome is "that which is conducive to Life itself."

Conversely, unintelligence produces unintelligent outcomes—those that are anti-Life, destructive, and degenerative.

Wars, corruption, injustice, greed, racism, pollution, and the systemic degradation of both humanity and the planet—these are all the products of a lack of true Awareness. A man who sees war as "necessary" or corruption as "just the way things are" is a man who is not truly Aware—his aperture is still narrow, his perception still dimmed by unconscious programming.

Thus, Awareness is not simply the act of "paying attention." It is the gateway to intelligence itself. It is what allows us to discern truth from illusion, wisdom from manipulation, and alignment with Life from actions that degrade and destroy it. The more Aware we become, the more we align with true intelligence, and the more our own actions, choices, and existence become life-affirming.

This is why Awareness is the first Siddhi. Before we can cultivate Presence, Character, Worth, or Contentment, we must first see clearly. For the man still asleep, none of the other Siddhis can take root. Awareness is the light that reveals where we stand, what must be changed, and how we must evolve. It is the first step toward self-mastery and the beginning of all wisdom.

THE MASCULINE PRINCIPLE OF STILLNESS & PERCEPTION

A man cannot cultivate true Awareness if he is constantly moving, reacting, or drowning in external noise. Awareness is born in stillness. This is a core principle of the exalted Masculine: the ability to hold presence, to be still, to observe before acting. The unawakened man, lacking Awareness, is always doing—chasing, reacting, grasping, struggling. He confuses motion for progress and activity for achievement. Yet without Awareness, all of his efforts amount to aimless thrashing in the dark.

The Masculine principle of Stillness & Perception is what grants a man his ability to see the truth of things—to penetrate beyond the surface appearances and discern the deeper reality beneath. It is the difference between the man who reacts impulsively to life and the man who responds with wisdom and clarity.

A truly Aware man does not merely see—he perceives.

To see is to look at something with our eyes. It is passive. But to perceive is to engage with full Awareness—to sense, to feel, to understand the deeper layers beyond the obvious.

A man who is Aware perceives the subtleties of human nature. He notices when a person's words do not match their energy, when someone is smiling but masking sadness, and when tension hangs in a room despite an outward appearance of harmony. He sees the hidden motivations behind actions, the patterns repeating in his own life, and the cause-and-effect relationship between his choices and his outcomes.

Awareness is what allows a man to sit in stillness and discern his next move with precision. It is what allows him to move through the world deliberately rather than being a slave to impulse, desire, or external pressures. This is why the exalted Masculine is synonymous with unwavering presence.

A man who lacks Awareness is easily manipulated, easily controlled, and easily deceived—by others, by the media, and by his own unchecked emotions and biases. A man of deep Awareness, however, is sovereign. He is immune to external manipulation because he sees clearly—he discerns truth from illusion, genuine leadership from deception, and wisdom from rhetoric.

This is why stillness is the first step to expanding Awareness. We must quiet the external noise, silence the incessant chatter of the mind, and create the internal spaciousness to perceive life clearly. The untrained mind will resist stillness, seeking distraction and stimulation. But the disciplined man understands that power is found in stillness. From here, he cultivates a presence that commands respect, an aura of discernment, and a depth that others instinctively recognize.

Stillness is not inaction. It is the foundation of all right action. It is the space where Awareness is born.

EXPANDING AWARENESS
From the Self to the World

Awareness begins as an inward journey. A man who lacks self-awareness cannot possibly be aware of the world around him in any meaningful way. His vision will be clouded by his unchecked biases, his unexamined traumas, and the limitations of his conditioning.

The first expansion of Awareness is, therefore, Awareness of self. This includes:

- Understanding our patterns—why we think, feel, and behave the way we do.

- Recognizing our emotional triggers—what sets us off
  and why.
- Identifying our subconscious beliefs—the programming
  we have absorbed from family, culture, and society that
  governs us without our conscious consent.

This stage of Awareness is often uncomfortable. It forces a
man to see himself clearly, including the aspects he would rather
ignore. But without this step, any attempt to expand Awareness
beyond the self is built on an unstable foundation.

Once a man has cultivated self-awareness, his perception
naturally expands outward. He begins to see the interconnectedness of all things. He recognizes that nothing exists in isolation—every action, every thought, every word has a ripple effect
that extends far beyond what the eye can see.

This is where Awareness moves from self-mastery to wisdom.
A man at this level begins to observe the world with clarity, seeing beyond appearances to the deeper currents shaping events,
relationships, and even history itself. He notices:

- The cycles and patterns playing out in human behavior,
  both individually and collectively.
- The invisible forces driving political, economic, and
  social systems.
- The hidden truths behind mainstream narratives,
  recognizing where manipulation and illusion are at play.

The expansion of Awareness is a gateway to true intelligence—not intelligence in the limited human sense of raw intellect or accumulation of facts, but the intelligence of understanding reality as it truly is.

With expanded Awareness comes heightened responsibility. A man who sees clearly can no longer claim ignorance. He is now tasked with acting from a place of wisdom. This is why many men unconsciously resist Awareness—they fear what they will be called to do once they see things clearly.

But the exalted Masculine does not fear Truth. He embraces it, even when it is inconvenient, even when it requires change, even when it forces him to stand alone. He understands that expanding Awareness is the only true path to sovereignty, wisdom, and mastery over his life.

This is why Awareness is the first Siddhi—it is the gateway through which all other higher capabilities emerge. Siddhis are not mystical gifts granted to the chosen few; they are latent powers within each of us that awaken through self-mastery. The Siddhi of Awareness grants a man the ability to *see*—not just in the literal sense, but to see into the nature of reality, into the deeper truths beyond illusions, and into the highest possibilities of his own *Being*.

From self-awareness to universal Awareness, this journey is the initiation into a life of higher intelligence, deeper perception, and unwavering truth. And as his Awareness expands, so does his potential to awaken the other Siddhis that lie dormant within him.

AWARENESS AS THE GATEWAY TO MASTERY

Awareness is the first Siddhi because without Awareness, none of the other Siddhis can be truly embodied at the level of true mastery. A man cannot fully embody Presence if he is unaware of his own distracted mind. He cannot truly access Character if he is blind to his own weaknesses. He cannot recognize his intrinsic Worth if he remains unconscious of the false narratives that diminish his self-perception. And he will never know true Contentment if he is unaware of the forces—both internal and external—manipulating his desires and expectations.

Thus, Awareness is the foundation upon which all other Siddhis emerge. It is the first great unlocking, the widening of perception that allows a man to see beyond the surface of things and into the deeper nature of reality itself.

A man who lives in deep Awareness moves through life differently. He is not easily deceived, for he sees beyond illusions. He is not reactionary, for he perceives the roots of conflict before they take hold. He is not ruled by his emotions, for he understands them and does not mistake them for absolute truth. He is not a victim of circumstance, for he recognizes the patterns of his own creation woven into the fabric of his reality.

But Awareness is not something we achieve once and then possess forever. It is a living Siddhi, an ever-expanding aperture through which we see reality. The more we develop it, the more it deepens, the more it refines our perception, and the more it gifts us with access to higher intelligence.

A man who fully embodies Awareness becomes a seer in the truest sense—not in the mystical sense of divination, but as one who sees reality as it is. He does not stumble blindly through life, nor does he cling to the false comforts of ignorance. Instead, he walks with clarity, steadiness, and the rarest of all gifts: the ability to discern truth in a world that constantly seeks to obscure it.

This is why Awareness is not just the first Siddhi—it is the keystone of an awakened life. It is the singular force that determines whether a man moves through life as a passive participant or as a master of his own destiny.

For those who cultivate Awareness, the path ahead becomes clear. They do not need rigid formulas or dogmatic teachings—they only need to see. For a man who truly sees will always know which direction to take.

And from this place, the next Siddhi—Presence—begins to emerge naturally, as Awareness deepens into a state of embodied *Being* rather than just perception.

The journey continues.

Once you see, you cannot unsee.

PRESENCE

DEFINING PRESENCE

P RESENCE IS MORE THAN JUST PHYSICAL PROXIM-
ity—it is a state of being, a force, a Siddhi that radiates
from within. A man can sit in the same room as another,
yet one's presence may be felt deeply while the other fades into
the background. This is because Presence is not merely about
where we are but *how* we are. It is the rare quality of being fully
engaged with life, undistracted, undivided, and completely
attuned to the moment at hand.

Presence is *embodied Awareness*. If Awareness is the ability to see clearly, Presence is the ability to be fully immersed in that seeing—to step into it, to integrate it, to *live* it. Presence takes Awareness from an intellectual concept into something palpable, something that can be felt by others in the field of a man who has truly mastered it. It is the Siddhi that transforms knowledge into wisdom and vision into action.

But Presence is rare. Most men are absent—not physically, but mentally, emotionally, and spiritually. They are tethered to the past, reliving old wounds or projecting into the future, chasing anxieties or desires that remove them from the power of *now*. The modern world encourages this absence, pulling attention in a thousand directions and training men to be everywhere except here.

A man who is Present, however, is an anomaly. He does not fidget, does not scan the room looking for something better, does not check out of conversations, and does not get lost in his own thoughts. He is there, fully, in a way that is unmistakable. His energy is *available*, and that availability makes him powerful.

Presence is the antidote to the scattered, distracted, and fragmented nature of most modern lives. It is the essence of true strength because it allows a man to meet life *as it is*, without flinching, without escaping, and without fear. It is what allows him to hold his ground in moments of chaos, to listen without immediately getting triggered and then needing to react from his own triggers, to move with precision rather than haste.

And this is why Presence is a Siddhi. It is not simply a habit or a practice, though those can help cultivate it. It is a rarefied state of being that, when fully embodied, exerts a gravitational pull. The world unconsciously seeks men who are Present—women and children are drawn to them, men respect his Presence, leaders emerge from them, and trust is placed in them.

Presence is not loud or forceful. It does not demand attention. Instead, it commands it in the most subtle yet powerful of ways—by simply *Being*.

THE POWER OF PRESENCE IN ACTION

A man who embodies Presence alters the energy of every space he enters. He does not need to announce himself; his mere existence commands attention, not by force, but by the unmistakable weight of his *Being*. This is the hallmark of a Siddhi—it is not something one does, but something one *is*. True Presence cannot be faked or imitated. It is not posturing, nor is it a performance. It is an emanation of deep inner alignment, of a man who has mastered his own mind and emotions to the extent that he no longer wavers in his *Being*.

The power of Presence reveals itself in how a man moves, how he speaks, and how he listens.

A Present man does not rush his words, nor does he speak to fill space. His pauses are intentional; his silences are weighty. When he listens, he does so completely—not just to the words being said but to the energy behind them. People *feel* when they are truly being seen and heard, and this is why a man of Presence naturally commands trust and respect.

In moments of chaos, Presence is a stabilizing force. When others panic, a man who has cultivated this Siddhi remains grounded, unwavering, and fully engaged with the reality of the moment. He does not react impulsively; he responds with intelligence and precision. Presence is what allows a man to hold the line when others falter, to remain poised when the world around him is unraveling.

But Presence is not just about strength—it is also about depth. It is the quality that allows a man to create profound connections, to be fully engaged in his relationships, and to make others feel valued. A man of Presence does not merely hear his Lover's words; he *feels* them. He does not just acknowledge his child's excitement; he *shares* in it. His relationships flourish because he is fully *there*—a rare and precious quality in a world where most are lost in their own distractions.

This is why Presence is magnetic. Women are drawn to it because it makes them feel safe and seen. Other men respect it because it signifies discipline and inner mastery. The world *gravitates* toward men who have cultivated this Siddhi because their Presence provides a rare oasis of safety and Order in an uncertain world that often feels unsafe and where Chaos reigns.

Ultimately, Presence is not something to strive for in isolated moments—it is a way of moving through life. It is a practice that deepens with every interaction, every breath, and every conscious moment. It is a Siddhi that, once fully embodied, becomes a man's signature—his silent yet unmistakable mark upon the world.

THE PATH TO CULTIVATING PRESENCE

Presence is not an innate gift bestowed upon a select few; it is a Siddhi that any man can cultivate with intention, discipline, and self-mastery. It requires a deep understanding that Presence is not about effort—it is about *allowing*. It is the shedding of distractions, the quieting of inner noise, and the full engagement with *this* moment—nothing more, nothing less.

The first step toward cultivating Presence is mastering one's own attention. Most men have scattered awareness—constantly pulled by thoughts of the past, worries about the future, or digital distractions that rob them of the now. A man of Presence trains himself to *be here*. He learns to direct his full awareness to the task at hand, to the person in front of him, to the experience unfolding in real time. He reclaims his mind from the endless chatter that weakens his ability to *be*.

Breath is a powerful gateway to Presence. A man who controls his breath controls his state of being. Shallow, erratic breathing is the mark of a scattered mind, while deep, steady breathing signals a man who is fully rooted in his body and aware of his surroundings. The breath anchors a man into the moment, into his physical form, and into the steadiness required for true Presence. This is why warriors, monks, and great leaders alike have always trained their breath—it is the key to mastery over one's state.

Stillness is another vital component of Presence. In a world of hurried movement, a man who is calm, composed, and unrushed *commands*. His stillness is not passive—it is potent. It communicates control, confidence, and certainty. He does not fidget; he does not seek escape. His body language, his posture, and his gaze all reflect an unshakable Presence that signals to the world: *I am here. I am undistracted. I am fully engaged.*

Yet, true Presence is not rigid—it is fluid. It allows for adaptability and spontaneity, but without losing center. A man of Presence moves *with* life, not against it. He listens deeply, not just with his ears, but with his intuition. He observes before he acts. He speaks when necessary, and his words land with weight because they are spoken from a place of full awareness.

Finally, Presence is a practice, not a destination. It must be cultivated in the mundane before it can be wielded in the extraordinary. A man does not wait for the battlefield or the boardroom to summon his Presence—he builds it in the way he pours his morning coffee, in the way he listens to his wife or child, in the way he walks into a room. Over time, Presence becomes his natural state—his baseline mode of *Being*.

Through this cultivation, a man rises beyond mere existence into a state of heightened *Being*. He becomes a living embodiment of the Siddhi of Presence—an unwavering force deeply connected to reality and in command of himself in a way that very few ever attain.

THE EMBODIMENT OF PRESENCE

Presence is not something a man does—it is something he *is*. It is not a skill to be occasionally applied; it is a way of *Being*, a fundamental shift in how he moves through life. A man who embodies Presence does not *try* to be present—he simply *is* because he has stripped away everything that pulls him away from the now.

This is why Presence is a Siddhi—it is not achieved through force or technique alone but through deep attunement to Life itself. When a man fully embodies Presence, he does not seek to dominate a room; his Presence does it for him. His energy does not shout—it resonates. His steadiness is not rigid—it is fluid. His stillness is not passive—it is powerful.

A man of Presence does not rush through life, nor does he cling to outcomes. He trusts the moment, and in doing so, he cultivates an effortless magnetism. Women feel safe in his energy as they sense his unwavering stability. Other men respect him, even without knowing why. The world responds to him, not because he demands it but because he embodies something rare—someone *fully here*.

PRESENCE AS A GATEWAY

Presence is a gateway through which all other Siddhis can become more fully expressed at deeper levels of purity. Without Presence, Character lacks depth, Worth remains unclaimed, and Contentment becomes fleeting. Presence is the key that unlocks a man's fullest potential, allowing him to not just *exist* in the world but to *inhabit* it fully, with his body, mind, and spirit in absolute alignment.

A man who has mastered Presence does not seek validation, nor does he chase after fleeting distractions. He is *here*—fully alive, fully aware, and fully in command of himself. This is why Presence is not merely a virtue; it is a power, a Siddhi that separates the mundane from the extraordinary.

And from this place of deep embodiment, the next Siddhi—Character—emerges naturally. For a man who has truly mastered Presence will find that the weight of his Character is no longer something he constructs, but rather it is something that radiates effortlessly from the depths of who he truly is.

Once you see, you cannot unsee.

SIDDHI #3

CHARACTER

THE WEIGHT OF TRUE CHARACTER

CHARACTER IS NOT ABOUT PUBLIC PERCEPTION, nor is it about conforming to the expectations of society. True Character is who you are when no one is watching, the unshakable foundation upon which your principles, values, and actions stand. It is not about appearing "good" but about being steadfast in what is right, even when the world pushes you to bend.

Most men claim to have values, yet few live by them when tested. This is because Character is not a declaration—it is embodiment. It is the difference between a man who speaks of honor and one who lives honorably. It is the dividing line between those who waver in the face of discomfort and those who remain resolute, unbending, and immovable, no matter the circumstance.

To possess the Siddhi of Character means to have an internal framework so strong that nothing external—whether societal pressure, fear of rejection, or desire for approval—can shake it. It is the quiet, unwavering force that commands respect without demanding it. A man of true Character stands firm in who he is. He does not seek permission. He does not compromise his essence. He does not fold when the world applies pressure.

Character is having a backbone, and a man without a backbone is easily swayed, manipulated, or broken. It is what separates those who merely drift with the current from those who shape the world around them.

THE TEST OF CONVICTION

Character is not proven in moments of ease—it is forged in fire. It is easy to hold strong opinions when there is no cost attached to them. But what happens when upholding your principles demands sacrifice? When standing firm means losing approval, opportunity, or comfort?

This is where the Siddhi of Character emerges—not as an intellectual concept, but as an embodied state of *Being*. A man of Character does not shift his values based on convenience. He does not compromise his integrity for short-term gain. He does not mold himself to fit into the expectations of others. Instead, he chooses his path with absolute clarity and walks it without hesitation, regardless of the obstacles before him.

A man's convictions are only as strong as his willingness to uphold them when tested. Many claim loyalty to Truth, but when faced with social rejection, professional consequences, or personal discomfort, they betray their own values. This is not Character—it is expedience.

Character demands that a man be willing to pay the price for what he believes in. The world will attempt to silence, sway, and dilute him. It will tempt him with compromise, with comfort, with easier roads. But Character is the refusal to kneel to anything less than the highest Truth known to him.

This is not born from arrogance or stubbornness—it is the deepest form of self-respect. A man of Character does not need external validation because his compass is internal. He is grounded in something unshakable. And because of this, the world around him recognizes his presence as something rare, something powerful—something untouchable.

OUR HEART
The Backbone of Character

True Character is not built in the Mind—its seat of governance is in the Heart.

The Mind, for all its brilliance, is a survival instrument. It seeks efficiency, comfort, and security. It rationalizes, negotiates, and often distorts reality to avoid discomfort. When faced with uncertainty, the mind recoils. When challenged by adversity, it looks for the easiest escape. The Mind, left unchecked, will choose convenience over conviction, compromise over courage, and self-preservation over principle.

But the Heart knows.

The Heart is where the lion within a man lives. It does not calculate risk in the same way the Mind does. It does not falter when challenged, nor does it shrink when confronted with difficulty. The Heart is unwavering—it beats with an ancient wisdom that transcends logic. It knows what is right. It knows what is true. And it does not bend, even when the Mind tries to convince us otherwise.

A man of Siddhic Character does not allow his Mind to rule over his Heart. He does not allow fear, doubt, or self-preservation to dilute his Truth. He feels deeply, but he does not let those feelings sway him from what he knows in his Heart to be right. His Heart is his compass, and his Character is the force that ensures he stays the course.

This is why Character is not about external validation or adhering to societal expectations. It is about an inner alignment with the highest Truth—a Truth that is felt, not calculated. When a man leads from his Heart, he becomes unshakable. He no longer needs external permission to stand in his integrity. He no longer seeks approval to be who he is. He is rooted, sovereign, and resolute.

The world will always test a man's Character. It will offer him easy paths and tempting compromises. It will challenge his convictions, seduce him with comfort, and push him to betray what he knows is right.

But the man who is centered in his Heart will not falter. He will not let fear govern his actions or convenience dictate his choices. He will walk the path of Truth, even when it is difficult, even when it is lonely, even when the entire world tells him to turn back.

Because that is what it means to be a man of true Character.

THE BACKBONE OF TRUE CHARACTER
It Takes Balls

True Character takes balls. It takes guts, fire, and an unflinching willingness to stand firm in a world that seems designed to strip men of their essence, dull their edges, and emasculate them into quiet submission. This isn't hyperbole—it's the stark reality. The world thrives on control, and nothing is more dangerous to the system than a man who cannot be manipulated, who lives by his own internal compass, and who refuses to trade his highest Truth for comfort, convenience, or approval.

A man of Character won't be castrated by the expectations of society, nor will he allow the forces around him to neuter his strength, conviction, or presence. And make no mistake—that's exactly what the world will try to do.

From the moment we're born, we're fed messages telling us to play nice, fit in, follow the script, and avoid rocking the boat. We're told to shrink ourselves, hide our fire, and swallow our Truth to make others more comfortable. But a man of true

Character knows that his mission is not to make the world comfortable—it's to live in alignment with what he knows is right, no matter the discomfort that arises in the process.

And it's not just the external world that seeks to castrate us—our own Mind is often complicit. It tries to seduce us into the illusion of safety, whispering that it's easier to stay quiet, to avoid conflict, to blend in. The Mind is wired for survival, and it will always nudge us toward the path of least resistance. But the Heart? The Heart roars with the Truth.

Again, Character lives in the Heart, not the Mind.

The Mind will lie to you to protect you from perceived threats. It will justify compromises, excuse cowardice, and rationalize dishonesty. But the Heart? It knows. It always knows. And when you follow your Heart, you tap into the raw, unfiltered power of your true nature—the lion within.

It takes balls to live from the Heart because the Heart doesn't take shortcuts. It doesn't bargain with fear. It doesn't dilute truth to make life easier. The Heart demands full commitment, and that commitment is the essence of true Character.

THE CASTRATION TRAP

The world fears men with Character because they can't be controlled. They can't be swayed by propaganda, coerced by fear, or distracted by trivialities. And so, the world attempts to castrate them—to tame their wildness, dull their instincts, and reduce them to passive, compliant shells of who they were meant to be.

This castration comes in many forms. It comes through the normalization of mediocrity, where men are taught to settle for lives of quiet desperation. It comes through addictions that numb the Soul—whether it's porn, alcohol, weed, gambling, sports voyeurism, consumerism, or endless scrolling on a screen. It comes through societal narratives that mock masculinity, diminish male strength, and paint true Masculine power as toxic or outdated.

But a man of Character doesn't fall for it. He sees the trap for what it is, and he refuses to let the world neuter him. He holds the line. He stays true to his values. He has balls, not because it's easy, but because it's who he is.

THE PRICE OF TRUE CHARACTER

Living with Character will cost you. It will cost you relationships with people who prefer you weak. It will cost you opportunities that require you to compromise your values. It will cost you the temporary comfort that comes from going along with the crowd. But what you gain in return is worth infinitely more.

You gain the respect of those who matter. You gain the peace that comes from living in alignment with your Truth. And most importantly, you gain the deep, unshakable self-respect that comes from knowing you didn't sell out, didn't cave in, and didn't let the world castrate you.

This is the Siddhi of Character—the ability to embody and uphold the virtues when tested and challenged, even in a world that does not always value and reward them due to its own misplaced values and priorities.

It's not about being perfect. It's about *Being* real. It's about having the balls to stand for what our Heart knows is right, speak Truth, and walk through life with the quiet majesty of a man who knows who he is and refuses to apologize for it.

And that kind of man? He can't be tamed. He can't be controlled. And he damn sure won't allow himself to be castrated by anyone.

THE ENDURING FIRE OF CHARACTER

In the end, Character is not something we inherit, nor is it something we can fake. It is forged in the fire of our choices, tested in the moments when standing firm costs us something, and revealed in how we walk through life when no one is watching. It is the quiet yet unbreakable force that separates men who merely drift through existence from those who carve their path with intention and conviction.

A man of true Character does not crumble under pressure, nor does he barter his integrity for approval. He walks his path with unshakable resolve, knowing that the world will attempt to soften him, tame him, and mold him into something more palatable. But he refuses to be diluted. He stands, spine straight and heart ablaze, anchored in his Truth.

This is why Character is not merely a virtue but a *Siddhi*—a mastery that transcends ordinary discipline and becomes an innate expression of *Being*. A man who has ascended into the Siddhi of Character *is* Character itself—unshakable, incorruptible, and sovereign.

The world does not need more men who conform—it needs more men who actually live their Truth. It needs more men of Character, men who possess the audacity to be steadfast in their principles and the courage to live with an undivided Heart.

Character is the ultimate test of a man's proclaimed convictions and higher Truth. And for those who cultivate it as a Siddhi, the rewards are beyond measure—a life of self-respect, trust, and an unshakable sense of purpose.

A man of Character does not merely exist, he stands for his own highest Truth.

Once you see, you cannot unsee.

WORTH

THE ILLUSION OF EXTERNAL VALIDATION

FROM THE MOMENT A BOY TAKES HIS FIRST STEPS into the world, he is conditioned to believe that his Worth is something to be earned, won, or proven. Society measures him by his achievements, by what he can *do* and *acquire*—status, wealth, accolades, influence. He is led to believe that his value as a man is tied to these external metrics, and that without them, he is somehow *less than*.

This illusion is reinforced in countless ways. As boys, we are praised when we perform well in school or excel in sports. As young men, we are validated by career success, financial gains, or the admiration of others. The message is clear: *you are only as worthy as what you produce, achieve, or possess.*

Yet, what happens when the promotions stop, the money dries up, or the applause fades? What happens when the game of validation no longer rewards him? For the man who has tied his sense of Worth to external things, this is an existential crisis. He feels hollow, unanchored—lost.

And this is where most men live. Even those who appear to have it all—power, wealth, status—often remain enslaved by the very things they chased. Their Worth is still conditional, dependent on the next success, the next victory, the next validation. They are never truly *free.*

This is the great deception. Worth is not something to be *achieved* in the Outer World—it is something to be *realized* in our Inner World. Until a man understands this, he will always be at the mercy of external forces, seeking approval, chasing validation, and fearing its loss.

But there is another path—the path of the Siddhi of Worth. A path where a man no longer *seeks* his value in the ever-changing world around him but instead *knows* it within himself. Where his Worth is unshakable, untouchable, and entirely his own.

THE SIDDHI OF TRUE WORTH

A man who embodies the Siddhi of Worth no longer looks outside himself for validation—he *knows* his value, not because of what he owns, accomplishes, or receives from the world, but because of *who he has become*. His Worth is not contingent upon circumstances or fleeting successes; it is an intrinsic recognition of his *Being*, rather than his *doing*.

The exalted Masculine does not question his Worth, because he understands that his true value is determined by the purity and authenticity of his *inner world*—his virtues, his Divine essence, and his unwavering commitment to embody the highest Truth accessible to him. He is not swayed by trends, nor does he seek permission from the world to affirm his existence. His self-worth is sovereign, standing independent of external validation.

This is where most men fall short—not because they lack ambition or capability, but because they fail to *anchor* their Worth in their immutable Divine essence of their inner core. If a man ties his value to his wealth, he will be broken if it is taken away. If he ties it to his physical strength, he will crumble with age. If he ties it to relationships, he will be lost when they change or end. But if he roots his Worth in the very fabric of his *Being*, in the embodiment of his exalted Masculine archetype and his highest known Truth, then nothing—literally *no thing* outside of him—can diminish it.

This is the paradox: the world tells men to *earn* their Worth in the Outer World, but the highest Truth is that true Worth is something a man can only *realize* in his Inner World. It is never given; it is never lost. It simply *is*. And once a man awakens to this, he becomes unshakable. He no longer asks, *Am I good enough?* He simply *knows*.

THE ILLUSION OF EXTERNAL WORTH

From the moment a man is born, he is conditioned to measure his Worth by external metrics—status, wealth, achievements, the opinions of others. He is taught that his value must be *earned* through success, power, influence, or material possessions. This illusion is deeply embedded in society, reinforced by cultural expectations, media narratives, and generational conditioning.

Yet, every man who has played this game long enough eventually comes to the same realization: *No external validation ever fills the void of self-doubt.* No amount of money, fame, or achievement can bestow true self-worth. It may provide momentary satisfaction, but it is fleeting—always leaving a hunger for more, always whispering, *You are only as good as your last win.*

This is why even the most outwardly "successful" men often feel empty. They have mistaken *egoic worth*—the value assigned to them by the world—for their *intrinsic Worth*, the eternal recognition of their divinity and purpose.

A man trapped in this illusion is easily manipulated. He becomes a slave to the game, constantly chasing the next achievement, the next approval, the next proof of his worthiness. He fears failure, not because of the failure itself, but because he has tied his Worth to outcomes that are never fully in his control.

The Siddhi of Worth liberates a man from this cycle. When a man realizes that his Worth is not contingent on *anything* outside of him, he becomes untouchable. He no longer seeks permission to feel valuable. He no longer fears losing what he has built. He no longer plays by the rules of those who would have him doubt himself.

This is the ultimate act of self-sovereignty: to step out of the illusion and *know*—with absolute certainty—that he is already whole, already enough, already worthy, simply because he *is*.

ANCHORING WORTH IN THE ETERNAL

To embody the Siddhi of Worth, a man must root himself in something that cannot be taken away. As mentioned before, if his sense of value is built upon things that are transient—his bank account, career, social standing, or even relationships—then his self-worth will always be fragile, vulnerable to the tides of his fortune.

But true Worth is immutable because it is not built upon *what* a man has but on *who* he is. A man anchored in his intrinsic Worth carries himself differently. He does not need to prove anything to anyone. He does not chase recognition, nor does he diminish himself to make others comfortable. He is simply *himself*—unapologetically, unwaveringly, and with a quiet certainty that cannot be shaken.

This certainty does not come from arrogance; it comes from an unbreakable connection to his Soul. He understands that he is not merely a product of this world but an expression of something greater, something eternal that transcends the material world. Hence, his Worth is not defined by external conditions because it is a reflection of his Divine essence—eternal, unalterable, and beyond question.

When a man reaches this level of deep knowing, it translates into embodiment, and when our true Worth becomes embodied, it becomes self-evident. He does not demand it. He does not seek validation. He does not need the world to tell him he is valuable because he *knows*—and that knowing radiates outward, drawing others into his sphere of influence effortlessly.

The world recognizes a man who is unshakable in his Worth. Not because he shouts it from the rooftops but because it is evident in everything he does. He moves differently. He speaks differently. He makes decisions from a place of sovereign confidence rather than fear or insecurity.

This is the power of the Siddhi of Worth—it cannot be gained or learned; it is *remembered*.

THE REVERENCE OF WORTH

When a man realizes his own intrinsic Worth, it does not end with himself—it becomes the lens through which he perceives all of Life. He no longer sees others through the distorted filters of status, wealth, or external accomplishments. Instead, he recognizes the innate Worth in every person he meets, independent of their position in society or the illusions of material success.

This realization extends beyond humanity—it awakens a reverence for the Sanctity of all Life. He sees the divine intelligence woven into every aspect of existence, from the smallest blade of grass to the vastness of the cosmos. He no longer views the world as something to extract from or dominate but as something to cherish and honor. In doing so, he aligns himself with the natural order, embodying a presence that uplifts rather than diminishes, that contributes rather than consumes.

A man who has embodied the Siddhi of Worth no longer seeks validation from the external world because he has already found it within himself. And in this state, he begins to embody the next Siddhi—*Contentment*—the final and most elusive state of *Being*, where the "void within" dissolves and the man stands complete, fulfilled, and at peace with himself and all of Creation in whatever form it appears in his reality.

Once you see, you cannot unsee.

CONTENTMENT

DEFINING TRUE CONTENTMENT

ONTENTMENT IS ONE OF THE MOST MISUNDER-stood states of being. Many mistake it for happiness, satisfaction, or the mere absence of suffering. But true Contentment is something far greater—it is the deep, abiding presence within us that remains untouched by the changing tides of Life itself. It is not about feeling "good" all the time, nor is it about avoiding hardship. Instead, it is the ability to rest in the fullness of existence, exactly as it is, without resistance, craving, or attachment.

Unlike happiness, which is often dependent on external conditions, Contentment does not rely on circumstances, achievements, or even emotions. It does not come from attaining desires, winning, or experiencing success in the Outer World. A man can have all the riches, accolades, and pleasures the world can offer, yet still feel an insatiable void within. Conversely, another man may have very little, endure hardship, or navigate the depths of personal trials, yet still carry an unshakable peace within his Heart. This is the mark of the Siddhi of Contentment—a state of being independent of conditions, rooted in something far deeper than anything the world can bestow or take away.

Contentment is *not* passivity. It is not resignation, complacency, or indifference. Some mistake it for a lack of ambition or the surrendering of desires, but nothing could be further from the truth. A man of Contentment is not one who has given up; he is one who has mastered the art of engagement with Life. He participates fully, strives where striving is needed, and embraces the experience of *Being* alive, yet he does so without inner turmoil, grasping, or resistance. He does not need the world to be different for him to be at peace.

This is why Contentment is a Siddhi. It is not something one simply chooses; it is a state that emerges when a man has transcended the Mind's endless pursuit of "more" and has come to rest in the natural perfection of Life itself.

CONTENTMENT AS THE STEADY STATE OF *BEING*

To truly grasp the Siddhi of Contentment, one must first understand that it is not an emotion—it is a state of being. Emotions, by their very nature, are transient; they ebb and flow like the tides. One moment, a man may experience joy, and the next, he may feel sorrow. The Mind constantly labels these emotions as "positive" or "negative," creating a cycle of attachment and aversion that keeps most men in a constant state of seeking or avoidance.

But Contentment exists beyond the turbulence of emotions. It is a quiet, unwavering steadiness—a subtle yet profound sense of peace that underlies all experience. Whether one is in the heights of triumph or the depths of despair, Contentment remains, like the stillness of the ocean beneath its waves.

This is why the Siddhi of Contentment is often described as a gateway to deeper states of spiritual realization. It is the foundation upon which true equanimity is built. A man who has cultivated this Siddhi does not suppress or ignore his emotions; rather, he recognizes them for what they are—passing phenomena, mere ripples on the surface of his deeper knowing. He feels fully, yet he is not enslaved by what he feels.

There is an immense power in this. Life's highs and lows do not easily sway the man who embodies Contentment. He does not require the world to conform to his expectations in order to feel at peace. He does not chase temporary pleasures in an attempt to escape suffering, nor does he crumble when faced with adversity. His peace is not conditional, for he has realized that true peace is not something found *outside* of himself—it is something he carries *within*.

CONTENTMENT AND THE INTELLIGENCE OF THE HEART

Contentment, as a Siddhi, is not something the Mind can achieve through logic or reasoning. The Mind is an instrument of measurement, contrast, and categorization—it is always evaluating, comparing, and seeking ways to manipulate circumstances to create a sense of control. But Contentment is not the result of external control; it is the product of deep inner alignment, which is accessed through the intelligence of the Heart.

The Heart does not operate in the domain of "if this, then that." It does not bargain for peace or calculate whether life is meeting its expectations. The Heart knows that Contentment is not dependent on conditions—it is an inherent state, always available, always present.

When a man learns to reside in his Heart, he steps out of the Mind's endless loop of craving and aversion. He stops chasing fleeting pleasures and running from perceived pain. He begins to understand that all experiences—joy and suffering alike—are simply facets of the same great unfolding. Nothing is truly "good" or "bad" in the absolute sense; all experiences serve a purpose in his Soul's evolution.

This does not mean he becomes indifferent or unfeeling. On the contrary, a man anchored in Contentment is more alive, more engaged, and more open to the full spectrum of life. He does not resist what is; he flows with it, embracing each moment as it comes, knowing that beneath it all, his essence remains untouched, unwavering, and deeply at peace.

Contentment, then, is not something a man must "achieve." It is something he must *allow*. It is a remembering—a return to what has always been there beneath the noise of the world and the chatter of the Mind.

CONTENTMENT AS THE GATEWAY TO WONDER AND REVERENCE

A man who embodies the Siddhi of Contentment begins to see Life itself through an entirely different lens. No longer caught in the relentless pursuit of more, no longer tormented by thoughts of what he lacks or what could have been, he instead discovers something unexpected—a deep, abiding sense of wonder.

Contentment is not stagnation; it is an awakening to the richness of life that was always present but often overlooked. When a man is no longer consumed by the Mind's endless grasping, his awareness naturally shifts to the beauty and depth woven into the very fabric of existence. He begins to notice the subtleties—the way light moves across the sky at dawn, the intricate patterns in a single leaf, the sacred silence of the night. Life itself becomes an unfolding masterpiece, not because anything has changed but because his capacity to *see* has expanded.

With this deeper awareness comes reverence. He no longer sees himself as separate from life but as an integral part of its great unfolding. He respects the sacredness of each moment, each experience, and each breath. Contentment brings him to a place where he no longer takes life for granted but rather experiences each moment with quiet gratitude.

This reverence extends beyond his own life. He begins to recognize the Worth of all beings, not in terms of what they produce or achieve, but simply because they *are*. He sees the interconnectedness of all things and moves through the world with a deeper sense of responsibility—not out of obligation, but out of Love (the energy). A man of Contentment does not seek to dominate life; he seeks to *honor* it.

In this way, Contentment is not a passive resignation—it is an active participation in the mystery of existence. It is not the absence of desire but the refinement of it. He no longer desires to control, to accumulate, or to manipulate life to fit his expectations. Instead, he desires to witness, to experience, and to *be* in harmony with all that is.

And in this, he discovers something extraordinary: the peace he once sought in the world was always within him. He was simply looking in the wrong place.

THE TRANSCENDENCE OF INDIVIDUAL LIFE

As a man masters the Siddhi of Contentment, something remarkable begins to unfold—his experience of life shifts from merely his personal experience to something far greater. He no longer sees himself as just an individual moving through the world, bound by his own story, ambitions, and struggles. Instead, he begins to experience Life itself as a force that flows *through* him, just as it flows through every other being, every blade of grass, every gust of wind, and every movement of the cosmos.

This is not the loss of self, nor does it mean that he dissolves into nothingness. Rather, it is the realization that his existence is not separate from the grand, unfolding mosaic of humanity. His individual journey is still uniquely his own, but it is no longer something he must desperately hold onto or define himself by. Instead, he sees his life as a vital and irreplaceable puzzle piece—one among many, yet essential to the whole.

From this vantage point, the ups and downs of his own personal life become far less significant in the grand scheme of things. He no longer defines his worth by fleeting successes or failures, nor does he seek validation through external measures. Instead, he is anchored in something far deeper—an unwavering sense of belonging to something infinite, something sacred.

This is where true Contentment reaches its highest expression. A man no longer fights against life, nor does he feel the need to mold it into his own limited vision. Instead, he becomes a vessel for Life itself, moving in harmony with its currents, embracing the unfolding of his path without resistance. He trusts not only in himself but also in the intelligence of the Universe, which is far greater than his Mind could ever comprehend.

He does not abandon his personal story, nor does he reject his human experiences. He still has goals, still loves, and still faces challenges, but now he does so with an effortless grace. He is no longer burdened by the weight of expectation. He moves forward with a quiet knowing that he is precisely where he is meant to be, that life is unfolding exactly as it should, and that *who he is*—at this moment—is already enough.

And in this realization, he finds the greatest gift of all: the freedom to *just be*.

THE QUIET TRIUMPH OF CONTENTMENT

The Siddhi of Contentment is not loud, flashy, or dramatic. It does not announce itself with grand victories or sudden epiphanies. Instead, it settles into a man's *Being* like a deep, abiding peace—an unshakable knowing that he is whole, that life is complete exactly as it is, and that nothing outside of him can add or take away from that truth.

A man who embodies this Siddhi moves through the world with effortless grace. He is neither restless nor complacent, neither clinging nor avoiding. He participates in life fully, yet he is unattached to outcomes. He experiences both joy and sorrow, yet neither defines him. He sees the changing tides of fortune and misfortune, of pleasure and pain, but he remains rooted in something deeper, something eternal.

Contentment does not mean a man stops striving, growing, or creating. It simply means he is no longer *chasing*. His drive is no longer fueled by a sense of lack but by the pure joy of expression, contribution, and service. He acts not because he must prove himself but because his heart overflows with the desire to give.

This is the final Siddhi, the state of *Being* that allows a man to rest in the fullness of himself and his place in the grand design of life. It is here, in the quiet triumph of Contentment, that he finds the greatest power of all—not in controlling the world, but in fully surrendering to it.

Once you see, you cannot unsee.

THE ATTUNEMENT

"I created a vision of David in my mind and simply carved away everything that was not David."

—MICHELANGELO

MASTERY—
PURUSHARTHA

ATTUNEMENT
The Final Refinement

ATTUNEMENT, IN A SPIRITUAL SENSE, REFERS TO bringing into harmony. In the context of this book, Attunement is the process of aligning one's Masculine essence with the 10 virtues and 5 Siddhis we have explored thus far. It is the final refinement—the alchemy that transforms theory into embodiment, knowledge into lived wisdom.

Through *The Curriculum* contained in this book, we laid the foundation of the ethos and operating principles of the exalted

Masculine archetype. Through the *Siddhis*, we expanded our conscious awareness of the exalted states of consciousness accessible to us. Now, through the *Attunement*, we bring everything into harmonic resonance, ensuring that our Masculine expression is no longer fragmented or inconsistent but fully harmonized—the exalted Masculine, embodied in every thought, word, and action.

THE PATH TO MASTERY AND
THE ANCIENT WISDOM OF PURUSHARTHA

In the Vedic tradition, the concept of *Purushartha* defines the four fundamental aims of human life. These aims offer a blueprint for living with purpose, providing a roadmap for spiritual fulfillment while honoring the realities of human existence. Arranged in their true order of priority, these four aims are:

1. **Moksha (Liberation)—The Ultimate Aim.** *Moksha* is the highest aim of human life—the transcendence of worldly attachments, the realization of our eternal nature, and the liberation from the cycle of birth and death (*samsara*). It represents the attainment of true wisdom, where the illusion of separation dissolves, and one aligns fully with divine truth. This is the pinnacle of the exalted Masculine archetype—the embodiment of full self-mastery, sovereignty, and spiritual enlightenment. *Moksha* is not an escape from life but rather the deepest

participation in it, free from ignorance, suffering, and false identification with the transient.

2. **Dharma (Righteousness & Moral Duty)—The Guiding Principle.** *Dharma* is the sacred duty, the righteous path that governs both individual conduct and the collective order of the universe. It represents living in alignment with higher principles—truth, justice, and honor. A man of the exalted Masculine follows his *Dharma* unwaveringly, regardless of external pressures. He does not compromise his values for expediency or personal gain. Instead, he sees *Dharma* as the guiding force that brings balance and harmony to his life and the world around him. Without *Dharma*, all pursuits—no matter how grand—ultimately lead to disorder and suffering.

3. **Kama (Sensory Pleasures)—The Enjoyment of Life.** *Kama* represents the legitimate enjoyment of sensory pleasures—love, beauty, passion, and the richness of human experience. Contrary to ascetic philosophies that reject pleasure, Vedic wisdom recognizes that joy and fulfillment are intrinsic aspects of life. However, *Kama* must always be pursued in accordance with *Dharma*. When pleasure is sought for its own sake, devoid of righteousness and wisdom, it leads to addiction, attachment, and suffering. But when experienced

through the lens of self-awareness and virtue, *Kama* becomes a sacred expression of the divine.

4. **Artha (Material Prosperity)—The Means, Not the End.** *Artha* pertains to the pursuit of material wealth, success, and economic stability. It acknowledges that financial security and resources are necessary to support oneself, one's family, and one's greater mission in the world. However, *Artha* was never meant to be the primary aim of life—it is simply a tool, a means to higher ends. In modern Western civilization, the priorities of *Purushartha* have been inverted, with *Artha* often positioned at the top. The relentless pursuit of wealth, power, and status has overshadowed the deeper spiritual purposes of life, leading to widespread emptiness, disillusionment, and moral decay. True mastery requires restoring *Artha* to its rightful place— not as life's purpose but as a resource to serve one's *Dharma* and facilitate the journey toward *Moksha* (spiritual liberation).

By internally realigning with the wisdom of *Purushartha*, a man opens up his pathway to true mastery—not only in the Outer World but, more importantly, in his Inner World. He recognizes that *Artha* and *Kama* are not destinations but instruments, that *Dharma* is the unwavering compass of his life, and that *Moksha* is the ultimate fulfillment of his highest potential.

In this alignment, a man walks the path of self-sovereignty, embodying the exalted Masculine with purpose, integrity, and transcendence.

THE INTEGRATION OF *PURUSHARTHA* INTO THE EXALTED MASCULINE

The exalted Masculine is not an abstract ideal; it is a lived reality forged through the conscious integration of *Purushartha* into one's *Being*. To walk this path is to embody mastery in all dimensions—physical, emotional, mental, and spiritual—while maintaining alignment with the higher order of Life itself.

Modern man, informed by the norms, values, and beliefs held within Western civilization, is conditioned by a culture obsessed with external validation and often finds himself in a misalignment where *Artha* and *Kama* dictate his pursuits, while *Dharma* (righteous action) is reduced to an afterthought (or violated) and *Moksha* (spiritual liberation) remains an elusive concept, if considered at all. However, the true path to self-mastery requires the inverse: anchoring oneself in *Dharma*, seeking *Moksha* as the highest aim, and allowing *Artha* and *Kama* to be conscious, intentional pursuits rather than unconscious compulsions.

A man who integrates *Purushartha* into his life embodies:

- **Unshakable Inner Order**—He operates with clarity and purpose, undistracted by societal noise or fleeting desires. His pursuits are guided by wisdom, not impulse, and he does not deviate from his *Dharma* for convenience, comfort, or mere personal gain.

- **Sovereignty**—He recognizes that external achievements are merely tools, not measures of his intrinsic worth. He is neither enslaved by the pursuit of wealth nor controlled by the fear of losing it.

- **Mastery of Desire**—He enjoys the pleasures of life without being owned by them. He understands that true fulfillment does not come from indulgence but from conscious engagement with life's experiences in alignment with his highest values.

- **A Life of Service and Transcendence**—His existence is not merely about personal gratification but about contribution. He recognizes that the highest expression of manhood is not dominance but upliftment—of himself, of others, and of the world around him.

This is the path of attunement, where the four aims of human life do not compete with one another but organically harmonize into a singular, exalted way of *Being*. Through *Purushartha*, the exalted Masculine archetype is no longer a concept but a lived embodiment of mastery, sovereignty, and transcendence.

HARMONIZING THE FOUR AIMS OF LIFE

A man walking the path of Attunement does not reject *Artha* (material prosperity) or *Kama* (pleasure), nor does he view *Dharma* (righteous action) and *Moksha* (spiritual liberation) as distant ideals reserved for monks or ascetics. Instead, he seeks to harmonize all four aims of life, recognizing that each has its place and function within his journey. True mastery does not come from the rejection of any aspect of life but from the rightful integration of all aspects into a coherent, elevated way of *Being*.

However, harmony does not mean equality. There are times when *Artha*—the pursuit of resources, stability, and material wealth—requires focus, such as when a man is building his foundation in the world. There are moments when *Kama*—the experience of pleasure, joy, and beauty—demands attention, especially in cultivating deep intimacy, artistic expression, or simply savoring the richness of life. Yet, these must never override *Dharma*, which serves as the guiding principle ensuring that *Artha* and *Kama* do not become unbridled indulgences that lead a man astray. And through it all, *Moksha*—the ultimate liberation—remains the North Star, the unseen yet ever-present aim that frames all other pursuits in the light of higher Truth.

A man who is attuned to this wisdom understands that *Artha* and *Kama* are tools—not masters. He seeks material wealth (*Artha*) not for hollow accumulation but as a means of supporting his higher mission. He engages in pleasure (*Kama*) not as an escape but as a pathway to greater connection, depth, and presence.

This is where the sacred dimension of *Kama* becomes significant. In the modern world, *Kama* is often misunderstood as hedonistic indulgence—an insatiable hunger for pleasure that leaves a man empty and enslaved. But in its higher form, *Kama* is a gateway to divine experience. This is evident in the ancient Tantric traditions, where the merging of the material and spiritual realms occurs through the sacred expression of pleasure. In the West, Tantra is often reduced to "tantric sex," but in truth, this is merely one practice within a vast and profound spiritual discipline that teaches the exalted union between the Masculine and Feminine as a means of touching the Divine. In its highest form, *Kama* is not about lust but about the deep reverence for the beauty and sacredness of embodied existence.

Thus, a man of attunement engages in *Artha* with responsibility, enjoys *Kama* with reverence, walks in *Dharma* with unshakable integrity, and moves toward *Moksha* with devotion. He does not sacrifice one for the other, nor does he cling to any single aim at the expense of the rest. Instead, he allows them to dance together—each taking its rightful place as he flows through the seasons of life.

This is the essence of attunement. It is not about rigid dogma or extreme asceticism, nor is it about unchecked indulgence. It is about mastering when and how to engage with each aim, ensuring that they serve his highest self rather than pull him into disharmony.

Through this integration, he does not merely seek mastery—he merges with it through attunement.

THE EMBODIMENT OF MASTERY
AND THE CALL TO BUILD

Mastery is not an endpoint but a living embodiment—an ever-deepening state of attunement between a man and the higher order of Life itself. A man walking this path faithfully and with inner conviction understands that *PurushArtha* is not a rigid doctrine but a dynamic interplay between the material and spiritual realms, one that requires continual refinement, wisdom, and self-honesty.

To integrate the four aims of life—*Artha, Kama, Dharma*, and *Moksha*—is to operate from a place of true sovereignty, where external success is no longer an unconscious compulsion but a conscious expression of alignment. It is to live with purpose, presence, and a deep knowing that all pursuits must be infused with integrity and higher awareness.

Yet, the exalted Masculine does not chase mastery just for mastery's sake, nor does he seek power for the sake of dominance. He understands that all he has cultivated—his virtues, his *Siddhis*, and his alignment with *PurushArtha*—is not meant to serve himself alone. It is meant to be extended outward, to shape and influence the world around him in constructive ways.

This is where the path naturally leads—to the creation of his Benevolent Kingdom.

Every man, regardless of his station, is building a Kingdom. Not all Kingdoms are equal as measured by titles, wealth, or power, but every man has a circle of influence—a space in which he governs, whether he is conscious of it or not. His family, his relationships, his career, his community, and even the unseen ripple effects of his presence in the world all form the foundation of his Kingdom.

The only question is: Will he govern wisely, with love, compassion, and integrity? Or will he neglect, abuse, or misuse the power and influence he has been given?

The next phase of mastery is not about what a man gains but about what he creates and builds in the world and how he governs his Kingdom. The great work of every man is not simply the attunement of Self—it's the extending his internal attunement with the higher principles of Life itself with his Outer World through the wise and benevolent stewardship of all he touches.

This is the worldly calling of the exalted Masculine: to step into his role as the benevolent patriarch of his Kingdom—not to claim power, control, or sovereignty over others, but of himself first, and then to be in service to his Kingdom and all that are touched by it, whatever its shape or size may be.

This is where we go next.

Once you see, you cannot unsee.

THE BENEVOLENT
KINGDOM

INTRODUCTION

EVERY MAN, WHETHER HE REALIZES IT OR NOT, IS the sovereign of his own Kingdom. His Kingdom is not defined by wealth, land, or status but by the realm of influence that he cultivates—the people he touches, the responsibilities he upholds, the standards he sets, and the way he shows up in the world.

Some men rule over vast empires, shaping industries, nations, or cultural movements. Others govern smaller realms—businesses, families, friendships, or communities. Regardless of the size of his dominion, every man has a Kingdom, and the way he governs it determines the legacy he leaves behind.

The Benevolent King governs not for his own gain but for the prosperity of his Kingdom, where prosperity is measured in the holistic well-being of all he touches, inclusive of material prosperity, but not just in the measure of the material wealth he creates and accumulates. He understands that true power is not in control but in service. His presence brings order, stability, and upliftment. He leads with wisdom, balancing strength with compassion, decisiveness with humility.

Conversely, the Narcissist Ruler rules not to serve, but to be served. His Kingdom exists as a mirror to reflect his own grandiosity. He seeks admiration, status, and personal validation, not responsibility. His leadership is hollow, driven by insecurity rather than true sovereignty.

The question is not whether a man has a Kingdom—the question is: How does he govern it?

Is he a steward of growth, harmony, and justice?

Or is he a slave to his own ego, governing through manipulation and self-interest? The path of the exalted Masculine is the path of the Benevolent King, but that path requires intention, wisdom, and attunement.

In this chapter, we explore what it means to build a Kingdom worth ruling, a legacy worth leaving, and a life of true sovereignty.

THE BENEVOLENT KING VS.
THE NARCISSIST RULER

At the foundation of the Benevolent King is love, compassion, and sacred duty—to himself, to others, and to the higher principles of Life itself. He sees his Kingdom as a direct reflection of his own embodiment of his virtues, and rising into the Siddhis of his exalted Masculine archetype allows him to gracefully assume his role as a steward of his Kingdom. His leadership is not rooted in self-interest but in service, knowing that true power is not about control but about creating an environment where all within his realm can thrive.

His actions are guided by wisdom, patience, and the deep understanding that power is a responsibility, not a privilege. He does not rule for validation, nor does he fear challenges because he knows that his strength is drawn from an internal source that is unshakable. His governance is built upon trust, fairness, and self-mastery—not because it is convenient, but because it is *right*.

By contrast, the Narcissist Ruler is guided not by love, but by fear, insecurity, and a wounded sense of self-worth. Beneath his bravado and lust for power is a man who is trapped in survival mode, seeing the world as hostile, dangerous, and adversarial. His leadership is reactive, not proactive. He does not seek to serve; he seeks to be *served*, believing that his power must be asserted through dominance, manipulation, and control.

Because his foundation is built on insecurity, he sees threats everywhere. He does not inspire loyalty through love; he demands obedience through coercion and emotional manipulation. He does not cultivate wisdom, for wisdom would require him to confront his own wounds. Instead, he builds illusions of grandeur, believing that more wealth, more titles, and more conquests will finally make him feel whole. But they never do.

Where the Benevolent King governs with strength and equanimity, the Narcissist Ruler operates from a place of lack, constantly seeking external validation to fill the void within. His fear of inadequacy becomes the shadow architect of his Kingdom, and instead of elevating those around him, he diminishes them—often without realizing that he is the very source of his Kingdom's decay.

In the end, these two archetypes do not simply govern and move through life differently; they view and experience life differently altogether:

- The Benevolent King walks in confidence, unshaken by adversity, secure in his purpose, knowing that his power is *not* in dominance but in upliftment. His Kingdom flourishes, and his legacy endures long after he is gone.

- The Narcissist Ruler walks in anxiety, consumed by his own shadows, driven by a perpetual hunger for control. His Kingdom may appear strong for a time, but it is built on fragile foundations, and inevitably, it will crumble beneath the weight of his own unchecked wounds.

Thus, every man must ask himself: Am I ruling my Kingdom with the wisdom, strength, and love of a Benevolent King?

Or am I imprisoned by the fear, insecurity, and hunger for control that marks the Narcissist Ruler?

Because in the end, it is not power or wealth that determines the quality of a man's expression into life—it is the state of his own Heart.

THE NARCISSIST RULER
Leadership by Domination

The Narcissist Ruler does not govern—he rules. His Kingdom is not a thriving ecosystem but a reflection of his fragile ego, a domain he seeks to control, manipulate, and bend to his will. His rule is marked by insecurity masked as dominance, by control disguised as strength, and by an insatiable hunger for validation that he mistakes for true power.

At the foundation of the Narcissist Ruler is not love, service, or sacred duty, but fear—fear of losing control, fear of inadequacy, and fear of being exposed as unworthy. He sees the world through the lens of scarcity and competition, where power must be seized and influence must be asserted lest he be overtaken. To him, those within his Kingdom exist to serve his needs, stroke his ego, and reinforce his sense of superiority.

Where the Benevolent King empowers, the Narcissist Ruler diminishes. Where the Benevolent King inspires trust, the Narcissist Ruler sows fear. His leadership does not create harmony but tension; his relationships are not built on mutual respect but on coercion, dependency, or intimidation. He confuses respect with obedience, mistaking the submission of others for genuine admiration.

But the Narcissist Ruler is never truly sovereign—he is a slave to his own wounds, perpetually seeking external validation to fill an internal void. He demands loyalty but does not inspire it. He seeks adoration in the form of Love (the energy) but does not know how to give it. He desires power but fears responsibility.

A Kingdom ruled by a Narcissist Ruler may stand for a time, but it is built on unstable ground. Its foundation is fear, its structure is ego, and its walls are made of fragile pride. In time, all such Kingdoms either collapse from within or are overthrown by those who recognize the hollowness of their ruler.

The Narcissist Ruler does not govern for the good of his Kingdom—he rules to avoid facing himself. And in doing so, he ensures his own inevitable undoing.

GOVERNING FROM THE SIDDHIS
The Benevolent King in Action

The Benevolent King does not rule by force or coercion—he governs with care, wisdom, discernment, and a deep sense of responsibility. His leadership is not reactive but intentional, forged through his unwavering commitment to embodying the exalted Masculine archetype. He understands that his Kingdom is not separate from him but is, in fact, an outward reflection of the deep inner work of initiation and purification he has devoted himself to.

His governance is rooted in the 10 Virtues, the foundation upon which his Character has been forged. Integrity, Discipline, Nobility, and Fortitude have strengthened his backbone, while Compassion, Temperance, and Valor have shaped his Heart. He moves through life with Wisdom, aware that his actions ripple far beyond himself, and he holds himself accountable to the highest standard—not because anyone is watching, but because that is the essence of who he has become.

Through the mastery of the Siddhis, he has sharpened his Awareness, embodying Presence in all that he does. His Character is unwavering, his Worth intrinsic, and his Contentment unshaken by the fluctuations of the Outer World. These Siddhis are not theoretical concepts to him—they are the lived experience of his *Being*. They infuse his leadership with a rare authenticity, a presence that others feel before he even speaks.

He also understands that his life must align with the great path of *PurushArtha*, the four aims of life. His Kingdom is not built on the blind pursuit of *Artha* (material wealth) or *Kama* (pleasure), as the Narcissist Ruler would prioritize, but is structured upon the foundation of *Dharma* (righteous action). His prosperity and enjoyment of life flow as a natural byproduct of his alignment with *Dharma*, while *Moksha*—liberation from the illusions of the false self—remains his highest guiding light.

This attunement between his Inner and Outer World allows the Benevolent King to govern with wisdom. He does not seek power for power's sake, nor does he govern to gratify his ego. Instead, he sees himself as a steward entrusted with the well-being of all within his realm. He does not extract from his Kingdom; he cultivates it. He does not manipulate or deceive; he uplifts and strengthens. He does not seek validation from the world; he leads because leadership is his sacred duty.

Above all, he understands that his Kingdom thrives because he thrives—not in superficial metrics of status or control, but in the depth of his wisdom, the purity of his Heart and intentions, and the unshakable knowing of the sovereignty of his *Being*. Those under his governance do not follow him out of fear but out of trust, respect, and admiration. They recognize in him something rare: a man whose power is not taken but earned through mastery of himself.

This is the essence of governing from the embodiment of the exalted Masculine archetype. It is not about ruling over others but serving them in alignment with the highest principles of Life itself. It is not about amassing wealth or influence (while that might very well happen organically) but building something enduring and meaningful. It is not about control but attunement—creating harmony between his Inner World and the Outer World he shapes.

This is the path of the Benevolent King, and it is the birthright of every man willing to walk the fire to get there.

THE NATURAL EVOLUTION
OF THE BENEVOLENT KINGDOM

A Kingdom, much like a man, is either evolving in a Life-affirming and regenerative modus operandi or devolving in an anti-life and degenerative modus operandi—it is never truly static. The Benevolent King understands that his work is never done, not because he is endlessly striving for more, but because the nature of Life itself is growth, evolution, and refinement. A Kingdom that is not evolving—spiritually, intellectually, relationally, and materially—is in decline.

But this evolution is not about expansion for expansion's sake. It is not about accumulating more land, power, or wealth to validate the King's sense of worth. Rather, it is about continuous refinement so that the highest Truths of his path of *ParashArtha* and Life itself are reflected within his Kingdom for the well-being of all in his care and all that he touches. The Benevolent King is not concerned with ruling over an empire—he is concerned with governing a Kingdom that remains aligned with higher Truths.

The Narcissist Ruler, on the other hand, mistakes expansion for evolution. He believes that more wealth, more status, more conquests, or more control is the sign of success, unaware that his Kingdom is built on unstable foundations. His fixation on external validation blinds him to the erosion happening beneath the surface. Where the Benevolent King nurtures long-term sustainability, the Narcissist Ruler sacrifices long-term stability for short-term gratification—leading his Kingdom to inevitable decay. His lust for status is insatiable because it is fueled by a void within that can never be filled by anything the Outer World has on offer. Hence, he does not cultivate a true Kingdom, he in the end merely consumes what has the outer appearances of a Kingdom.

A Kingdom that is governed through the Siddhis, the virtues, and the wisdom of *PurushArtha* will always be regenerative in nature, enriching all who exist within it. It is not bound by size but by depth. Whether a man governs a vast enterprise, a close-knit family, or simply himself, the principle remains the same: If his Kingdom is in harmony with Life's higher order, it will flourish.

The Benevolent King is always in attunement with the natural order of Life. He does not govern from ego, nor does he impose his will with force. He observes, he discerns, and he adjusts—ensuring that his Kingdom remains in a continuous state of refinement and elevation. He understands that his role is not to dictate outcomes but to steward the evolution of his realm in alignment with the highest principles of Life itself.

A Benevolent King's Kingdom expands not because he chases power but because his very *Being* emanates stability, wisdom, and sovereignty. People are drawn to him not out of obligation but out of trust. His influence is never forced—it is the natural byproduct of his inner attunement.

Thus, the greatest work of the Benevolent King is not external expansion but inner refinement. As he continues to embody the exalted Masculine archetype, his Kingdom flourishes as a direct reflection of his self-mastery. His presence becomes the foundation upon which all else is built.

THE LIVING KINGDOM

A man's Kingdom is not something he builds once and then presides over with complacency. It is a living reflection of who he chooses to be in every moment. Every conversation, every decision, every action—each is an opportunity to either govern wisely or rule from ego.

This is the last realization of the Benevolent King: His Kingdom is not built in the past, nor does it wait for him in the future—it is here, right now, always in a state of creation in the present moment.

The only question is: Who is he *Being*?

Does he create, build, and govern from the bedrock of his exalted Masculine archetype? Or does he fall into the grasp of self-doubt, fear, and limiting beliefs, pushing his power into the hands of external forces or the malware-infested default programming in his subconscious Mind?

This final question leads us to the closing chapter of this book—the realization that a man is never merely "Becoming" something; he is "*Being*" something in every single moment.

And it is his choice—always, each and every moment.

Once you see, you cannot unsee.

BEING VS. BECOMING

THE ILLUSION WITHIN BECOMING

MANY MEN LIVE UNDER THE ILLUSION OF Becoming—that our highest self, our power, our mastery, our sovereignty exist somewhere in the future, waiting for us when we've "arrived."

We tell ourselves:

- "We will be disciplined when we have more time."
- "We will be confident when we achieve more success."

- "We will be leaders when others recognize our worth."
- "We will be ready to step into our power when we've learned more, earned more, or prepared more."

But this thinking is a trap—a carefully constructed lie of the subconscious Mind designed to postpone sovereignty, postpone responsibility, and postpone action.

The problem? That future version of ourselves does not exist. The men we imagine ourselves to "become" will only ever remain a fantasy unless we choose to simply *Be* him right now in the present moment.

The Mind—conditioned by social programming, past failures, and deeply ingrained fears—will always find a reason why we are "not yet ready." It will feed us narratives that excuse inaction, promising that a better version of ourselves is "just around the corner."

But there is no corner. There is no future moment when we will suddenly be ready, worthy, or whole. The only moment is now, and therefore, the only real question is: Who are we *Being*, right now?

The exalted Masculine does not wait. He chooses. He decides. He embodies. Right now. Not when it's comfortable. Not when it's convenient. Not when the world grants permission.

Because in every moment, we are not "becoming" anything. We are *Being* something. The only question is—what?

We must ask ourselves the toughest question of them all: Are we at this very moment *Being* the man we know we could be?

Or are we waiting for the right conditions, delaying our own mastery, convincing ourselves we are still Becoming? Or worse, are we telling ourselves we are not "there" because of forces and circumstances outside of us?

Mastery is not something we achieve later. It is the sum of who we are *Being* in this very moment, and the next, and the next.

The men who wait die waiting. The men who decide live in their Power.

This is the very illusion within Becoming; when we decide we're still Becoming, that's who we are *Being*.

The path forward is simple: *Be* it now.

THE POWER OF *BEING*

All of Life only ever happens in the present moment. The past is a collection of memories shaped and filtered by our perception, and the future exists only as a projection of our imagination. Yet, so many of us live our lives trapped in these illusions— replaying old stories, regretting past choices, or anxiously constructing a future that never arrives. But reality? Reality is always *now*.

Our power to create, to act, to shape our reality exists solely in the present moment. *Being* is not something we can do in the past, nor is it something we can delay until some imagined future. It is only ever an expression of who we are in this exact moment.

If the illusion of Becoming keeps a man trapped in waiting, the power of *Being* liberates him into action. To truly embody the exalted Masculine, a man must shift his orientation from one of perpetual striving toward one of immediate presence, knowing that mastery is not something he will reach—it is something he must *Be* in every moment.

This is where true attunement begins.

Being is not passive. It is not the absence of ambition, nor is it complacency. *Being* is an active, engaged, and fully embodied state. It is the willingness to meet life as it is, to respond with clarity and strength, and to make each moment an expression of one's highest values.

When we are *Being*, we are not waiting to become.

We are not waiting to become wise—we are moving through life with wisdom.

We are not waiting to become strong—we are acting with strength.

We are not waiting to become worthy—we are standing in our worth without needing proof from the world around us.

To truly *Be* is to claim sovereignty over our own existence, to strip away the false stories that say we must wait, prepare, or prove ourselves before we can embody the man we know we were born to *Be*.

This is not about perfection. There will always be moments when we falter, when doubt creeps in, when old patterns try to pull us back into Becoming. But the difference is this—when we are *Being*, we recognize these moments for what they are: passing waves on the ocean of our consciousness. We do not let them define us. We do not let them dictate our actions. Instead, we return, again and again, to the present moment, to the choice that is always before us:

Who am I *Being* right now?

When a man commits to this question as his guiding principle, his life transforms. He stops waiting for the conditions to be right. He stops seeking external validation before he acts. He stops postponing his ascension into his own Power.

He steps into it.

This is the beginning of true attunement. This is the doorway to a life not spent in pursuit of mastery but lived as an expression of it.

THE FINAL REALIZATION
Attunement as the Ultimate Way of Being

A man walking the path of attunement is not striving to become something greater—he is choosing, moment by moment, to *Be* that which he already is at his highest potential at the highest octave available to him in that very moment.

He is no longer caught in the illusion that mastery is somewhere in the distance, waiting for him once he has "done the work." Instead, he realizes that mastery is in the very act of showing up in alignment again and again, no matter how imperfectly.

We will falter. We will fail. We will make mistakes. But none of this invalidates who we are *Being*—unless we allow it to. The difference between the man lost in Becoming and the man who fully embodies *Being* is not perfection but commitment. The man of *Being* recognizes that he can fall and rise in the same breath. That he can misstep but still remain steadfast on his path. That he can be both flawed and sovereign, imperfect yet unshakable.

Attunement, then, is not an achievement—it is an ongoing act of devotion. It is the conscious, moment-to-moment harmonization of his unique expression of the Masculine archetype with the virtues, Siddhis, and higher principles we have explored throughout this book. It is the choice to live our Truth rather than merely aspire to it.

In the end, there is nothing more to wait for. No permission to seek. No validation to chase. No milestone to reach before we step into our full expression. There is only one question we must ask ourselves right now and in every moment that follows:

Who am I *Being*?

In the end, that is the only thing that will have mattered because all any man creates, builds, or accumulates in his Outer World are, in the end, just sandcastles that the cosmic ocean of time will wash away.

But while the tides of time will erase all that we build in the Outer World, all that we cultivate within—the virtues we embody, the Siddhis we attain, the sheer mastery we gain in the expression of our *Being* on the canvas of all of Creation—these are ours to keep, carried forward beyond this lifetime, woven into the eternal journey of our Soul's evolution.

Once you see, you cannot unsee.

CLOSING REMARKS

Let me begin by saying this—this book, like any teaching, is not the finish line. It is merely a jumping-off point. No book, no philosophy, no system of wisdom—no matter how profound—can ever capture the totality of all there is.

The words and concepts contained within these pages are simply transmissions—fragments of understanding that the Mind can process, analyze, and synthesize. But the true transmission is unseen; it exists between the words, beyond the structure of language. It is energetic in nature, a resonance that calls forth something already present within you.

Even so, all this book can truly do is open a doorway—an invitation into the depths within you that have yet to be explored. I can show you the way, but only you can cross the threshold. You must now walk the path, take what serves you, and—most importantly—go beyond this book. No teaching is ever complete, no book is ever all-encompassing, and no teacher is ever all-knowing. Master what has been shared here, then transcend it.

Now, let's talk about Rome.

First, Rome wasn't built in a day. If you've read this book and feel an urgency to "arrive," let that go. Mastery takes time. True embodiment is not achieved in one day, one year, or even one lifetime. Enlightenment is not a sprint but an eternal unfolding, an evolution spanning lifetimes. There is no need to rush in an infinite game that has no finish line.

For those preoccupied with making this their "final" lifetime or wondering if they are close to "completing" their journey, my advice is simple: minimize the mental real estate you allocate to such thoughts. There is no harvest in it. As long as you are on this side of life, you are here to engage in it fully—not to speculate on its conclusion.

Second, all roads lead to Rome. The teachings within this book present one way—one path toward the exalted Masculine. But it is not the only way. There are many roads, many expressions of universal Truth, and many ways to find your way home. Choose the path that resonates with your deepest knowing, that stirs something undeniable within your Soul.

What matters is not the road you take but that you embrace the unwavering commitment to walk it.

THE JOURNEY AHEAD

As we reach the final pages of this book, let me emphasize once again: this is not the end. It is the beginning. Every word you have read, every insight that has sparked something within you, is merely a signpost—pointing toward the path you must now decide to walk.

The virtues, the Siddhis, the path of *PurushArtha*—these are not abstract concepts to be admired from a distance. They are invitations. Invitations to embody, to practice, to integrate, and ultimately, to transcend.

No man is born into mastery. Mastery is earned—step by step, choice by choice, moment by moment. And at its core, the highest mastery is not found in control, dominance, or perfection—it is found in attunement. Attunement to your own highest potential. Attunement to the deeper Truths of existence. Attunement to the creation of harmony between the Inner World and Outer World you experience as your reality.

This book has given you a framework, including guiding principles and a roadmap to navigate by. But no framework, no set of principles, no roadmap—no matter how profound—can walk the path for you. That responsibility is, and always will be, yours alone.

Now, as you set sail on this path in earnest, you will inevitably falter. You will inevitably fail. You will inevitably stumble into old patterns and wrestle with your shadows. But that is not what defines you. What defines you is whether you rise again and again. Whether you choose in each moment of difficulty to realign, to recalibrate, to recommit.

This is the high mark of the exalted Masculine. Not flawlessness, but relentless devotion to the highest Truth.

And in this devotion, you will discover something profound: the path itself is the reward. The man you transcend into along the way is the greatest treasure you will ever possess.

So go forward—not as someone who is merely learning or improving, but as someone who is choosing, moment by moment, to Be his highest version available in that moment.

And when the world tests you, when you feel yourself wavering, when the weight of life threatens to pull you back into unconsciousness, remember this:

You are not here to play small. You are not here to be ruled by fear, doubt, or convenience.

You are here to embody your highest expression so the ripple effects of your spiritual poetry may uplift and beautify our world in ways only your unique poetry can.

The world is thirsting for it. I steadfastly believe in it. But in the end, the only thing that matters is that you choose it—for yourself, first and foremost.

I see you, and the view is magnificent.